# Out of the Comfort Zone

## Vision, Grace, Action

D1037776

# Out of the Comfort Zone

Vision, Grace, Action

**George Verwer**

**OM**
**publishing**

Copyright © 2000 George Verwer
First published in 2000 by OM

Reprinted 2000

06 05 04 03 02 01 00    8 7 6 5 4 3 2

OM Publishing is an imprint of Paternoster Publishing,
PO Box 300, Carlisle, Cumbria, CA3 0QS, UK
and Paternoster Publishing USA
Box 1047, Waynesboro, GA 30830-2047
www.paternoster-publishing.com

**British Library Cataloguing in Publication Data**

A catalogue for this book is available from the British Library

ISBN 1-85078-353-5

Unless otherwise stated, Scripture quotations are taken from
the HOLY BIBLE, NEW INTERNATIONAL VERSION
Copyright © 1973, 1978, 1984 by the International Bible
Society. Used by permission of Hodder and Stoughton Ltd.
All rights reserved. 'NIV' is a registered trademark of the
International Bible Society
UK Trademark number 1448790

Cover design by Diane Bainbridge
Typeset by WestKey Limited, Falmouth, Cornwall
Printed in Great Britain by Omnia Books Ltd, Glasgow

# Contents

# Acknowledgements

I want to acknowledge the work of Falcon Green who listened to so many of my message tapes in order to put this book together with other articles I had written.

I also want to acknowledge Vera Zabramski and Hilary Price for the enormous amount of time they put into further changes and editing.

And I want to thank those thousands of people and hundreds of books and articles that have had such a powerful influence in my life.

I especially want to thank Billy Graham, my spiritual father, through whose preaching I discovered life and life in abundance.

# Foreword

George Verwer took me out of my comfort zone over forty years ago. As fellow students at Maryville College, in the hills of Tennessee, we met together from time to time to pray. After one of George's typically fiery passionate, loud prayers, I began a rather phlegmatic prayer. I was stunned when in the middle of my prayer he suddenly stood up and shouted, 'I got it!' I asked, 'George, what do you got?' His answer: 'We should go to Mexico in the summer.' That was the first time he had mentioned Mexico to me and he wanted an immediate positive response. I said I would have to pray about it.

We were quickly back on our knees and a few minutes later he again put the question to me, 'Well, are you ready to go?'

'George, it takes longer than that.'

I'll never forget the pained look on his face as he lamented, 'Why does it take people so long to see it?'

I did 'see it' and I did go. I saw it as a strictly one-off trip with George and Walter, another Maryville student. This mission would be short-term. Since I was planning to transfer soon to Wheaton College, I expected my friendship with George, and Walter would also be short-term. Maybe we would never see each other again. That's life.

That was September 1956 and we have been close friends and colleagues ever since. George is still in regular contact with Walter.

Long-term relationships – that's what I think of when I think of George. He is in touch with a number from those Maryville College days and from just about every other chapter of his life.

In January 1960 I attended George and Drena's wedding. George invited me to speak at the reception after the main ceremony. It is the only time in all these years that George has rebuked me for my preaching. I had unwisely divulged to the wedding guests that George would probably give away all the gifts they had brought and so beautifully wrapped! George questioned the appropriateness of my comments - but he did give away many of the gifts!

Let me give you just one example of what George did with his earthly possessions in those days (why do I say 'in those days'? He hasn't really changed all that much over these years.) While preaching in a small church in greater Mexico City, he was overwhelmed by the generosity of a collection that was taken. It was not so much money but he knew the people had given sacrificially. The pastor accompanied George to his van to say good-bye. George asked the pastor if he had a suit. 'No', he replied.

George responded, 'I have plenty of clothes.' It was night and the pastor could not see what was going on . George took his suit off, handed it to him and drove off. It was quite a sight to see a young skinny George Verwer in his under-wear around midnight knocking on the door of the Christian bookshop where the team was staying!

George and Drena's wedding was special. Even more beautiful was their fortieth anniver-sary celebration. As I looked around at the sev-eral hundred people there, I saw Ph.D.s and ones who had only the most modest education. There were the wealthy and the poor. There were leaders of major Christian organizations, as well as individuals who did not profess any form of Christianity. There were those who were apparently very successful in their pri-vate and public lives, there were also some who found coping with life just beyond their reach. We all had one thing in common. We were George's friends – long-term friends, that is.

Other pictures come to mind when I think of George. He is a risk-taker. He loves to live on the edge. You might say that his comfort zone is breaking out of his comfort zone. He only really feels secure when he's risking it all.

Apart from frequently riding the wildest roller-coasters, which he thoroughly enjoys, George's risks do have some greater purpose to them. Since coming to know the Lord through a gospel that a praying woman sent him and the preaching of Dr Billy Graham, his one all-consuming passion in life has been to be a channel, whereby people would become long-term friends of Jesus. To be such channels, George maintains, we have to leave our comfort zones. So be prepared for some new challenges as you let George share his vision through this powerful book. In the midst of it all you will be encouraged and ministered to by God's long-term grace.

Like it's author, *Out of the Comfort Zone* dodges no bullets and ducks no issues. This is a major challenge for Christians of the twenty-first century. One last word, coupled with George's passion is a commitment to balance. I appreciate the wisdom God has given George on a number of pressing issues that face missions today.

*Dale Rhoton*

# Introduction

This book is written for Christian leaders and especially servant leaders who long for greater reality in the whole Body of Christ. It also is written for anyone who is hungry for God and wants to understand better what God is doing and wanting to do across the world.

I am hoping that young people, who would be willing to be leaders in God's great kingdom-building programme, will read it. And I hope it will be read by thousands of former OMers and prayer partners who have stood with us in the work over so many years. I believe it will give a greater vision of that which burns in my heart in these days.

I wrote a proverb years ago that I have often quoted in meetings. It always gets a laugh because people know it is true:

Where two or three of the Lord's people are gathered together, sooner or later there will be a mess.

We, however, have a great and sovereign God who specialises in working in the midst of a mess.

We see this all around us and also from Genesis to Revelation. The Word says, 'This treasure is in earthen vessels' and we must face the implications of that. I often refer to it as 'The Human Factor' and much of it is a result of our sin.

As I write this introduction, my wife and I have just celebrated our 40$^{th}$ wedding anniversary and about 450 people came together here in the UK where we live, to give thanks to the Lord and to celebrate. I'm very aware that without my wife Drena, I would not be writing this book. Together we have been involved in the task outlined in this book for over four decades and we continue to grow in grace and knowledge of Him in the midst of weaknesses and struggles. We are still learning 'His grace is sufficient and His strength is made perfect in weakness'.

This book is a plea for reality, the kind of reality we see expressed in the life of Jesus and in the passages of His Word. It is my prayer that we will be driven deeper into God's Word with all its mystery and paradox and that we will learn more about what is really God's priority.

It is often easier to over-emphasize the 'distinctives' that divide us rather than the biblical basis of the faith that unites us. As we get involved in missions, and remember missions is people, we will have our hearts broken many times. If we don't want to be hurt, we have a real problem because living on this planet, as Billy Graham once said, 'Life at its best is full of sadness'. To be able to forgive those who have truly hurt us is one of the very basic principles of this great spiritual revolution.

*George Verwer*

# ONE

# A Grace-Awakened Approach to Missions Work

## Grace and its enemies

One of the main reasons I decided to write this book was to give a heart's cry for a 'grace awakening' in the area of missions work. This term, 'grace awakening', comes from the title of Charles Swindoll's book, *The Grace Awakening*, which has spoken so powerfully to me and many thousands of others over the past years. The book begins with a reminder that Christians are saved by faith through the sacrificial death of our Lord Jesus Christ on the cross and that we have nothing to offer Him in return. We can simply accept His free gift given to us in grace. Swindoll says, 'Once we grasp its [grace's] vertical significance as a free gift from God, much of horizontal grace – our extending it to others – automatically falls into place.'*

It is this 'horizontal grace' that I want to write about in this chapter – the quality that allows us to recognise that individual Christians and groups of Christians, including our group, are free in Christ from legalism, to grow and work as He leads us. 'It is for freedom that Christ has set us free. Stand firm, then, and do not let yourselves be burdened again by a yoke of slavery' (Gal. 5:1).

We rejoice in this freedom, but we do not flaunt it. We use it to build up others and show them respect in their walk with God and their work for Him. 'You, my brothers, were called to be free. But do not use your freedom to indulge the sinful nature; rather, serve one another in love' (Gal. 5:13).

Many spiritual writers have emphasised the same message. Stanley Voke's *Personal Revival*, is another book which has spoken powerfully to me of this truth of grace, along with Roy Hession's *Calvary Road*, which has been recommended reading in Operation Mobilisation since the very early days. These and many other books point us back to Scripture where great passages like 1 Corinthians 13 and

---

* Taken from *The Grace Awakening* by Charles Swindoll, © 1990 Word Publishing, USA, all rights reserved. Used with permission.

Ephesians 4 show us how to live in relationship with one another.

> Love is patient, love is kind. It does not envy, it does not boast, it is not proud. It is not rude, it is not self-seeking, it is not easily angered, it keeps no record of wrongs. Love does not delight in evil but rejoices with the truth. It always protects, always trusts, always hopes, always perseveres (1 Cor. 13:4–7).

> Be kind and compassionate to one another, forgiving each other, just as in Christ God forgave you (Eph. 4:32).

Another word that I sometimes use for this quality is 'big-heartedness'. I think of the incident recorded in the gospels of Mark and Luke when John reports to Jesus how the disciples stopped someone who was casting out demons in Jesus' name, but who was not one of them. John took the narrow, legalistic view but the account goes on, ' "Do not stop him," Jesus said. "No-one who does a miracle in my name can in the next moment say anything bad about me, for whoever is not against us is for us." ' (Mk. 9:39–40). Jesus took the big-hearted view.

The familiar verse, Romans 8:28, is another one of the 'big-hearted' scriptures, 'And we know that in all things God works for the good of those who love him, who have been called according to his purpose.' We often use this

verse to encourage ourselves or others we are
close to, when things do not seem to be going
well, as a reminder that God's compassion still
surrounds us. But of course we can also apply it
to others when we believe things are going
'wrong' for them because they aren't acting
correctly, or they are following policies and
strategies we don't agree with.

There is such a need for this grace-awakened,
big-hearted approach in mission work. There
are so many areas where a lack of grace causes
hurt and tension and positively hinders the
work of God across the globe. So often our
fellowship as Christians seems to be based more
on minor areas in which we are like-minded,
than on the real basics of the gospel and the clear
doctrines of the Christian faith which are so
amazing and on which we should be more
united.

Swindoll powerfully lists the enemies of
grace as:

> . . . from without: legalism, expectations, tradi-
> tionalism, manipulation, demands, negativism,
> control, comparison, perfectionism, competition,
> criticism, pettiness and a host of others; and
> from within: pride, fear, resentment, bitterness,
> an unforgiving spirit, insecurity, fleshly effort,
> guilt, shame, gossip, hypocrisy, and so many
> more . . . grace killers, all!

I think of all the people who have been rejected, to some degree, because they did not fit in with someone else's expectations – because they were not Baptists or Anglicans or because they did not speak in tongues, or did not come up to the mark on any one of a hundred possible issues, which may or may not be of genuine importance. Many have felt rejection and hurt because they were not received by those who emphasised the gifts of the Spirit, simply because they did not have the same understanding of those gifts. The reverse is also true. Those who emphasise the gifts of the Spirit have felt rejected by members of the body who didn't.

What makes this problem even more complex is that so often preachers emphasise these smaller issues from the pulpit, affecting how their congregations think and how they evaluate other people and their beliefs. It seems to me that our behaviour often testifies that these little issues are more important to us than the unity and reality that we have in Jesus Christ by the new birth through His Holy Spirit. We lack grace in this area.

## Speaking graciously about our work and the work of others

One of the areas where lack of grace shows itself to be most harmful is in the supposedly factual statements which people from one group – a church, a para-church organisation or a missions agency – make about those from another, without first of all checking that we have the facts straight and that we have the whole picture. Often, again, it is the leaders of organisations who make these kinds of statements. From my own 40 years of experience I realise that we can easily say negative things, however subtle, about other leaders or their ministries. Sometimes these comments lack a factual basis, which leads to false conclusions and generalisations. Sometimes, even when perhaps the facts are correct, they are put over in a way that is hurtful and damaging.

Constructive criticism, following the pattern of Matthew 18, is something quite different.

'If your brother sins against you, go and show him his fault, just between the two of you. If he listens to you, you have won your brother over. But if he will not listen, take one or two others along, so that "every matter may be established by the testimony of two or three witnesses." If he refuses to listen to them, tell it to the church; and if he refuses to listen even to the church, treat him as you would a pagan or a tax collector.' (Mt. 18:15–17).

I confess it is a great struggle to find the balance between telling the truth openly and boldly and acting with love. I think that often those of us in leadership don't realise how much extreme or untrue statements upset other leaders who hear them. Once they get into print or on e-mail and go around the world, it is almost impossible to correct them. If we are grace-awakened and love the Lord, then we will be more careful about all that we say or write about others.

In our present society, commitment to telling the truth is under threat. When we do say something that is not true it takes grace to confess and put it right. An inability to do this leads to a cover-up. If you think that there are no 'Watergates' in the Christian world, then I'm afraid you are in for a big shock!

The law in most countries is that you are innocent until proved guilty, but sometimes in the Body of Christ, you are guilty until proved innocent. May God have mercy on us for this habit. If we are to see great victory in these confusing days, then we must listen to one another and try to keep communicating with one another with grace. This is true in mission activities, in our local church and indeed in our marriages and all personal relationships.

Along with graceless criticism often goes a tendency to make exaggerated claims, again without sometimes having the facts right. Many are confused and even angry when they hear another Christian boasting; however, few have the love and courage to call that person to account and ask for more specifics about what is being stated. How extremely sad that the term, 'evangelically speaking', has come to mean that something is an exaggerated statement or statistic. Any effort we can make in reporting numbers more accurately would be a great victory for those involved in mission work.

For example, when a TV or radio station talks about a potential audience, we make a huge mistake if we report that audience as the number who actually watched or listened to a particular programme. And surely we must all finally agree that a decision or profession of faith doesn't necessarily mean a true, new Christian. Someone once said that if all the claims about his country were true, then everyone in the nation would have been converted twice! If we hold our listeners in esteem, then we are more likely to be careful with the facts.

On the other hand, people who are angry or offended by the exaggerations or wrong statements of other missions leaders, must not 'write them off' without any discussion or confrontation. If they know something of reality, brokenness and the way of the cross, they will be very slow to condemn or speak evil of another brother or sister, especially a leader in God's work. At the same time those making strong-minded statements or apparent exaggerations must be more approachable and willing for correction. They must also be more diligent in their preparation and research and make an extra effort to stick to the facts. They will have to learn to love their critics and resist making unkind statements about them in their ministry.

In the chapter entitled, 'The Grace to Let Others Be', Charles Swindoll identifies two powerful tendencies which nullify grace in people's dealings with one another. The first is the tendency to compare, of which he says:

> Before we will be able to demonstrate sufficient grace to let others be, we'll have to get rid of this legalistic tendency to compare. (Yes it is a form of legalism.) God has made each one of us as we are. He is hard at work shaping us into the image He has in mind. His only pattern (for character) is His Son. He wants each one of us to be unique . . . an individual blend and expression unlike any other person.

The second is the tendency to control. Swindoll says:

> Controllers win by intimidation. Whether physical or verbal, they bully their way in as they attempt to manipulate us into doing their will. . . . Whatever the method, controlling, like comparing, nullifies grace. If you are given to controlling others, grace is a foreign concept to you.

The opposite of grace awakening is the human tendency to be legalistic, narrow-minded and rigid, which is so often partly a cover-up for our own insecurities and fears. To be honest, I believe in some sincere saints it is actually a wrong view of Scripture, linked with over-emphasising favourite verses rather than the whole counsel of God.

It is amazing how some churches that I knew 20 years ago, born out of a new freedom of the Spirit, with lots of new ideas and strategies, are now more rigid in certain ways than the older churches they left in search of grace, freedom and reality. If you try to confront some of these new (now older) leaders about this you will see in their attitudes that history does repeat itself.

Don't we have 2000 years of proof that God works in a variety of ways? Different missions have different strategies and even within a mission or church there can be tension and division over strategy and the detail of how things should be done. Must we be so dogmatic on matters that the Bible is not clear about? Can't we accept that God works in different ways among different groups of people? The work of God is bigger than any fellowship or organisation. To get a job done we need organisations that respond to specific needs. For example, God brought Operation Mobilisation into existence for a specific purpose – to mobilise the young people of Europe and North America and then across the globe. We don't worship organisations or get uptight because we don't agree with everything in them. We should assess them in the context of their specific purpose and be big-hearted about them. Remember the message of Philippians 2, that we should esteem others as better than ourselves? 'Do nothing out of selfish ambition or vain conceit, but in humility consider others better than yourselves. Each of you should look not only to your own interests, but also to the interests of others.' (Phil. 2:3–4).

Wouldn't the practical implications of this bring a revolution of love and grace? It would mean that, as well as being caught up in the plans, goals and strategies of our own organisations, as of course we must be, we would become bigger-hearted, understanding more of the full picture of what was happening and the unity in the Body of Christ. What a wonderful day it would be if we were to hear mission leaders speaking out in a positive way about other people's plans, goals and strategies. How wonderful it would be to hear Christian writers and artists promoting other people's work and not just their own, taking other people's books and materials to their meetings. I thank God for those who already do this.

Esteeming other groups and individuals as better than ourselves would involve more than just speaking out on their behalf. It would include one group getting under the burden of another and assisting them positively with money, practical resources, know-how and prayer. There is a balance to be kept here because of course each mission group has its own God-given vision and methods and we must not pretend that there is unity where there isn't and insist on it when it isn't necessary. Neither must we use this as a cop-out and deny that Scripture requires us to esteem one another and act in grace towards one another, as God does to us.

## Grace where there's genuine disagreement

So, we need a grace awakening in the way we speak about one another, in the way we report the progress we are making in the work of taking the gospel to the world, in our practical approach to one another's work and in our sensitivity to one another's cultural and theological differences. But, we also need grace within the many genuine debates in the church over the best way to operate as we work to fulfil the Great Commission. So often the alternative ways of doing a job in missions are presented as incompatible, as 'either / or', instead of, 'either or both'. There are many of these controversies and some of them will be dealt with later in this book when I look at the debates over the relative value of tentmakers and full-time professional missionaries, whether missions should ask for money or not and whether to send missionaries from 'Western' countries or to concentrate resources on 'national' workers.

In all these debates my plea is for a 'grace-awakened' approach which gives esteem to the ways other people do things, which does not compare or control, which does not say, 'This is the only way' and which does not judge an organisation outside the context of its specific purpose. Where there is genuine disagreement, let there be loving and constructive discussion and even, sometimes, loving and constructive confrontation. Let us be honest about our differences. As Christians with a commitment to take the gospel to the world, we will of course sometimes have genuine disagreements. On some occasions there will be the need to take a hard line. Sometimes I wish Christians would take a harder line on issues such as the Ten Commandments, the doctrine of salvation by grace alone and the need to respond to the Great Commission, just to mention three examples. Where co-operation is not possible on central issues, we should have the grace to disagree lovingly and then get on with our work.

At this point, I want to look at a particular controversy in the world of missions as an example of how a grace-awakened, big-hearted approach could help to show the way forward. This is the disagreement over who makes a suitable candidate for certain types of mission

work. In today's church, there is great controversy over the word 'apostle' and of course
churches and denominations who use this term
must do so as they feel led without condemning
those who do not. In some circles it refers only to
a relatively small number of highly gifted and
qualified people. This way of thinking encourages the view that only the very best candidates
should be considered for mission work. I am in
full agreement with the practice of selecting
mission candidates with care, but the long history of the church shows that God sends out and
uses all kinds of people with a huge range of
gifts and talents. Stephen Gaukroger, in *Why
Bother With Mission?*, says:

> The history of missions is a colourful history of
> 'unlikely heroes' – characterized by obedience
> rather than ability. Time after time God confirms
> his word; 'Think of what you were when you
> were called. Not many of you were wise by
> human standards; not many were influential; not
> many were of noble birth. But God chose the fool-
> ish things of the world to shame the wise; God
> chose the weak things of the world to shame the
> strong' (1 Cor. 1:26–27).

Modern, short-term mission agencies have
often received people at a young age, with no
real mission experience. On-the-field
mentoring, the method used by Jesus, has

proved to be one of the very best ways to produce long-term church leaders and missionaries out of such people. Some assume that if we have a large number of new, especially young, workers that they will not be well-qualified workers. My experience has shown me, and I love to testify to the truth of this, that God uses all kinds of people. Books like *Ragamuffin Gospel* make this point and are well received by Christians in general but sadly, when a 'ragamuffin' senses that God is leading him or her to be a missionary, they suddenly find that many start to get very concerned about the quality issue.

At nineteen, I was one of those 'ragamuffins' who God somehow led and sent to Mexico. Today, why are there so many pouring cold water on young people and others who may not be 'apostles' (according to some people's definition), but who want to move out and serve God? Somehow perfectionism has got married to legalism and together these two can now stop even the most sincere and zealous disciple from taking steps of faith in the area of missions. Martin Goldsmith, in *Don't Just Stand There*, maintains, 'Missions do need highly qualified people, but they also need good people who may not have high academic or professional qualifications. Missions desire to work amongst people of all sorts, so they need workers of every experience and background.'

Let us older and supposedly more mature leaders acknowledge that many of the so-called 'quality' people of our generation have been knocked out of the battle or fallen into serious sin. The really big mistakes and sins that cause grief to the Body of Christ, in ways that are hard to assess, are not usually those of some inexperienced, young person on a short-term mission trip following a call to mobilise. As God's people we need to be more compassionate and concerned for our youth. Instead of condemning their music or the way they dress, we should be reaching out in grace and love. We should not compare what we think our strong points are with their weak points, but rather we should face our own weak areas more realistically and learn to let love cover their weaknesses. In this way we may begin to recognise the tremendous energy and commitment which they are able to bring to the work of taking the gospel to those in need.

In *The Grace Awakening*, Charles Swindoll entitles one of his chapters, 'Graciously Disagreeing and Pressing On'. In many ways this is a perfect description of the approach I have been trying to encourage to the controversies referred to in this and following chapters. Swindoll says:

One of the marks of maturity is the ability to disagree without becoming disagreeable. It takes grace. In fact, handling disagreements with tact is one of the crowning achievements of grace.

He goes on to quote Ephesians 4:29–32 – fitting words to end a chapter on the need for an awakening of grace in mission work. I quoted verse 32 earlier but look now at the whole passage:

> Do not let any unwholesome talk come out of your mouths, but only what is helpful for building others up according to their needs, that it may benefit those who listen. And do not grieve the Holy Spirit of God, with whom you were sealed for the day of redemption. Get rid of all bitterness, rage and anger, brawling and slander, along with every form of malice. Be kind and compassionate to one another, forgiving each other, just as in Christ God forgave you.

While writing this book, I started to read *What's So Amazing About Grace?* by Philip Yancey (winner of a 'Book of the Year Award' from the Christian Publishers Association). I urge you to read it as part of your pilgrimage to be a more grace-awakened person.

### Suggested reading:

Swindoll, Charles R., *The Grace Awakening* (Word Publishing).

Yancey, Philip, *What's So Amazing About Grace?* (Zondervan Publishing House).

Voke, Stanley, *Personal Revival* (OM Literature).

Hession, Roy, *Calvary Road* (Christian Literature Crusade).

Luther, Martin, *Commentary on Galatians* (Fleming H. Revell/Chosen Books).

## Books referred to:

Goldsmith, Martin, *Don't Just Stand There* (IVP).

Manning, Brennan, *The Ragamuffin Gospel* (Multnoma).

# TWO

# We Are His Witnesses

## Called to witness

This is how Stephen Gaukroger defines a cross-cultural missionary in his book *Why Bother With Mission?*

> One who is commissioned and sent out by his or her local church to cross cultural boundaries in order to be a witness for Jesus Christ. These boundaries may be those of language, geography, or society. He or she would also intentionally:
>
> - introduce people to Christ by his or her life, attitudes, actions and words.
> - seek to introduce those who come to Christ to join with others in the fellowship of a church. A church will need to be planted if it doesn't exist!*

---

\* Taken from: *Why Bother with Mission?* by Stephen Gaukroger, IVP. Used with permission.

Why should you, or anyone else, take up the challenge of this kind of missionary work? Why should we bother with mission? This is not the same as the question, Why do we need more missionaries? Nor is it the same as the question, How do you encourage *others* to get involved in mission? The question, Why should *I* be involved in mission? is something else altogether because it involves a personal, Spirit-led, God-centred decision about the direction of your own life. Such a decision is complex and I would never want to suggest otherwise.

What has to be faced up to, ultimately, is the fact that God, through His word, tells us that we are to be His witnesses. The challenge of the 'Great Commission' is given in Matthew 28:18–20, Mark 16:15, Luke 24:46–49 and in different terms in John 20:21–23. Acts 1:8 is also a vital scripture in this context. Read it carefully. ' "But you will receive power when the Holy Spirit comes on you; and you will be my witnesses in Jerusalem, and in all Judea and Samaria, and to the ends of the earth." ' This verse tells us that we are to be witnesses for Christ, to build the kingdom, where we happen to be ('Jerusalem') and in the whole world ('to the ends of the earth'). This suggests to me that we should start out as witnesses now, regardless of the geography of our situation. Stephen Gaukroger says:

So the Bible points us to the priority of mission with a relentless logic and a passionate enthusiasm. The nature and activity of God the Father, the work and words of God's Son and the example of the early church empowered by the Holy Spirit are clear. The Holy Spirit goes on applying the Scripture to our lives as we bring ourselves under its authority. We are commanded to be activists in the cause of mission, right up to the return of Jesus, preparing for the great destiny which awaits us. Fundamentally, the Bible affirms that our Christian faith is a mission-faith; if it isn't we ought to question whether it is biblical faith at all.

There is a 'being' and a 'doing' side to witnessing. Like so many things that people are arguing about in the church today, it isn't a case of 'either/or' but of 'both'. A. W. Tozer puts it like this:

Were human nature perfect there would be no discrepancy between being and doing. The unfallen man would simply live from within, without giving it a thought. His actions would be the true expression of his inner being.

With human nature what it is, however, things are not so simple. Sin has introduced moral confusion and life has become involved and difficult. Those elements within us that were meant to work together in unconscious harmony are often isolated from each other wholly or in part and tend to become actually hostile to each other. For this reason symmetry of character is extremely difficult to achieve. (*The Root of the Righteous*)*

A godly, holy life of love and integrity, no matter what a person's vocation, is a powerful witness in itself. However, the book of Acts and the history of the church show that to be a witness is also to speak out boldly about Jesus Christ. John Grisham's book, *The Client*, showed that being a witness to a murder can get dangerous and complicated. We know that this is also the case when we attempt to be faithful witnesses to the death and resurrection of the Lord Jesus Christ. My heart yearns for clarity and simplicity about this. Let us be careful, as we get into mission strategy, that all its complexity doesn't intimidate us. The emphasis in the book of Acts on boldness should help us to speak out – to remember the 'doing' as well as the 'being' side of witnessing.

For many Christians this is not a contentious issue. They understand that they should be witnesses within their locality, where their home or their job happens to be, living godly

* Taken from: *The Root of the Righteous* by A. W. Tozer, 1955, 1986 Camp Hill, PA: Christian Publications. Used with permission.

lives and speaking to others about Jesus. Many have a burden for the needy areas of their own land, the great cities perhaps. Meanwhile there has been a lack of emphasis on the 'ends of the earth'. There is a tendency to think that other people are looking after this.

Some are so burdened by the needs that surround them that they are unable to lift their eyes to other parts of the world. Some, especially in the traditional missionary-sending countries, are positively ill-informed and they oversimplify a complex situation by saying that Western missionaries are no longer needed or are no longer 'cost-effective' and that support for indigenous workers should replace the sending of people. Some people and groups have become distracted by the idea that only narrowly defined, so-called 'high quality' people are needed on the mission field, when in fact people of all kinds are needed to fill a huge range of jobs. Many have been desensitized by powerful media images and words so that they are no longer able to grasp the needs of distant places when simply told about them. Only by being there and feeling and smelling for themselves will they understand the need. (This, incidentally, is one of the reasons why I believe short-term mission work, despite its risks, can be so valuable in awakening understanding of the needs of the 'ends of the earth'.)

So the lack of emphasis on the the 'ends of the earth' may be understandable, but we cannot ignore the clear promise and command which our Lord gave in the passage from Acts quoted above. Scripture is clear – that our responsibilities do not end with 'Jerusalem'. The Apostle Paul emphasised the need to move on to those unreached:

> It has always been my ambition to preach the gospel where Christ was not known, so that I would not be building on someone else's foundation (Rom. 15:20).

> . . . so that we can preach the gospel in the regions beyond you. For we do not want to boast about work already done in another man's territory (2 Cor. 10:16).

## The power to witness

As we respond to the command of the Great Commission we should not forget the promise which it contains: '. . . you will receive power when the Holy Spirit comes on you . . .' A true witness experiences the power of God. The Bible makes it very clear that the strength to live the Christian life comes from the Lord, 'But we have this treasure in jars of clay to show that this all-surpassing power is from God and not from us' (2 Cor. 4:7).

This power does not necessarily mean we will experience great wonders in miracles and healing. Some people seem to feel that if these signs and wonders are not present, then there is no power. This is not the case. At the same time, it is clear in the book of Acts that the Holy Spirit will give boldness. We must try to avoid getting into extremes about this, believing that some perfect formula (such as the presence of some supposedly authenticating sign) will allow us to do all sorts of things that we have never done before. The key is to see the Holy Spirit as the One who makes the decisions about how missionary work should be conducted.

Acts 1:8 also promises us that witnesses will be filled with the Holy Spirit. Sadly, I believe that extreme and off-balanced ideas about the Holy Spirit and sanctification have confused and discouraged many people. We tend to forget that however filled with the Spirit we may be, there is still the 'human factor'. We are ordinary people who struggle, make mistakes and have weaknesses. I have become more and more convinced that God fills and uses different types of people, many of whom may not look very promising by 'normal' standards. When I was a young Christian I had a tendency towards extremism and 'super-spirituality'. If I had not learned to accept the 'human factor' in myself and others, I would have been knocked out of the race very early on.

If you are discouraged by your humanness in the face of the Great Commission, overwhelmed and paralysed by the size of the challenge, then consider for a moment Paul's approach to his weakness expressed in 2 Corinthians 12:8–10.

Three times I pleaded with the Lord to take it away from me. But he said to me, 'My grace is sufficient for you, for my power is made perfect in weakness.' Therefore I will boast all the more gladly about my weaknesses, so that Christ's power may rest on me. That is why, for Christ's sake, I delight in weaknesses, in insults, in hardships, in persecutions, in difficulties. For when I am weak, then I am strong.

The same Paul, who was so greatly used and whose heroic story we can follow through the book of Acts, had the same sense of weakness and he, by the guidance of the Holy Spirit, gave us these encouraging words.

## Going on after discouragement

As we respond to the challenge of the Great Commission, encouraged by the promise that we will be given power as we are filled with the Holy Spirit, there are two ways of thinking and acting which we need to cultivate. The first is the determination to get up and go on after discouragement. We have to accept that, as we get involved with missions, there will be mistakes, failures and sins. Although we should be sorry for them, rather than being intimidated by them and allowing them to corner us into inaction, we should use them as springboards to launch us into greater things for God. I once saw a book with the title, *Failure: The Back Door to Success*, by Irwin Lutzer. What an amazing book! To be honest, I never read it, but the title really did speak to me. Ragamuffins, despite all their efforts, do fail, and sometimes even break promises. The Bible shows us the right attitude to this kind of sin (not, of course, that all failure is sin): 'My dear children, I write this to you so that you will not sin. But if anybody does sin, we have one who speaks to the Father in our defence – Jesus Christ, the Righteous One.' (1 Jn. 2:1).

One of the most important aspects of walking with Jesus is to learn this lesson of how to bounce back when we fail. Surely this is what Hebrews 12:7–11 is talking about:

> Endure hardship as discipline; God is treating you as sons. For what son is not disciplined by his father? If you are not disciplined (and everyone undergoes discipline), then you are illegitimate children and not true sons. Moreover, we have all had human fathers who disciplined us and we respected them for it. How much more should we

submit to the Father of our spirits and live! Our fathers disciplined us for a little while as they thought best; but God disciplines us for our good, that we may share in his holiness. No discipline seems pleasant at the time, but painful. Later on, however, it produces a harvest of righteousness and peace for those who have been trained by it.

If we walk with God He will discipline us through our failures for our good. These are serious words but beware in all of this not to take yourself too seriously. Learn how to laugh at yourself while keeping on.

I remember clearly a great failure in my own life, in 1961, through which God disciplined me. I was living in Spain but I was studying Russian because my great vision was for the Muslim and Communist worlds. In the summer of 1961 I headed for Moscow with a vehicle full of well-hidden scriptures. I had such a great vision. You have heard of Brother Andrew, known as God's Smuggler: I was God's Bungler! The summer ended with us being arrested by the KGB, and the Russian newspapers reporting, 'American spies caught'. After a couple of days' interrogation, they decided we were religious fanatics and gave us a sub-machine gun escort to the Austrian border. It was after that fiasco, in a day of prayer, that the bigger vision and idea came to me with the name 'Operation Mobilisation'. Once again, by

God's grace, in the midst of failure, something great was born that was to explode spiritually across the world.

After failure, do you sometimes feel you have missed Plan A for your life? If you do, then thank God for His sovereignty and the reality of Romans 8:28: 'We know that all things work together for good for those who love God, who are called according to his purpose.' Plan B or C can be just as great as Plan A. You may think that you have made a lot of mistakes and taken a lot of wrong turnings in your life. Perhaps you feel you are on Plan F or G. I say, 'Praise God for a big alphabet' and press on! No matter how many heartbreaks, disappointments and difficulties there may be, we need to keep a positive, grace-awakened attitude and keep moving forward in our response to the call of Jesus to be His witnesses throughout the world.

## Being proactive

A second positive mindset we need to cultivate is that of being proactive. This is an approach which involves deciding and acting. The word 'proactive' is written on every page of the book of Acts. Many of God's people are drinking too much of that old depressing cocktail of perfectionism, introspection and false expectation, which has led to a new form of spiritual navel gazing, totally out of step with the kind of reality which we hear about in the book of Acts. C.S. Lewis said that we have the tendency to think, but not to act and to feel, but not to act. If we go on feeling and thinking, but not acting, then one day we will be unable to act. 'Are you waiting for some kind of call before you move out to find your strategic niche in God's global plan?' ask Bob Sjogren and Bill and Amy Stearns in *Run With the Vision*. They answer:

> Wait no more. We as God's people have been very clearly commanded, commissioned, called. We are to align our lives with the objective of making follower / learners of every people – including our own. In Old Testament parlance, we're to bless every people group – gracing them with the privilege of joining God's family through redemption in Jesus Christ.

Let us turn away from inaction and cast ourselves on the Lord in a new way, realising afresh all that we have in Christ. Remember that in Him are hidden 'all the treasures of wisdom and knowledge' (Col. 2:3).

There are subtle forms of discouragement against taking action. In some places today there is a strong emphasis on revival. With this emphasis can come considerable confusion and extreme ideas of what it will be like. People speak of the great revivals of the past, but sometimes they don't tell the whole story. Often when there is a special time of this kind there is also a counter-attack from Satan. In my experience throughout the world, an over-emphasis on revival leads to a subtle form of extremism and a 'copping out' from the basics of obedience, discipline and action-taking. If revival hits your church or region or university, there will be more intense spiritual warfare the very next day. There may even be greater heartbreaks and disappointments than there were before it came. There is no substitute for daily denying self and taking up the cross, regardless of your circumstances. To think that a great revival or spiritual experience will make Christian living a kind of 'automatic pilot' experience, is to make a huge mistake. Created as we are in the image of God, He has given us a free will and we are fully responsible for making the right decisions and taking the right steps on a moment-by-moment basis.

Some people are temperamentally more proactive than others. Some Christian people are worried by the possibility that there may be evidence of life in rocks that came in the form of meteorites from Mars. They are asking whether it will weaken faith in God if life is found on another planet. The only question which my proactive temperament makes me ask is, 'How much will it cost to hire a spaceship to reach these new forms of life with the gospel?'

Meanwhile we have quite enough to get on with here on this planet!

The Great Commission is more than a call for you or me to leave where we are and go somewhere else. There is of course a great need for people to go, but there is a greater need for each of us to take up our own responsibility as part of the church's response to the Great Commission: to be personally involved in it whatever our particular role may be. Let me illustrate this. One of my heroes in the world of mission work today is the son of a wealthy businessman who is putting big money into world missions and helping to build the kingdom. He goes on short-term missions and really catches the vision, especially for unreached people. When he gets home he shares his vision with his father who is aging and unwell. The father pours out his heart about the problems of the business and asks the son to step in and help for a few years. It's a hard decision, but the son takes on the job, in order to keep the funds going out to missions work, allowing others to continue with their work.

The point of this illustration is not that we have to copy this particular pattern of going and sending but that we need to respond to the Great Commission. We need to act in the most strategic way we can to play our part in its fulfil-ment, whether as a person who goes, as one who sends others or, as in the case of this man, one who does both. In short, we need to take ownership of the Great Commission for ourselves and look to God to guide us as to what our particular part in it will be.

## Counting the cost

To put your life, future and career on the altar for the Lord of Glory is no small affair. Luke 14 tells us that we must count the cost of what we do. For those who do go, there are distinct costs to be counted. There are four warnings I often give to people who are considering missionary work:

- Firstly your heart will be broken many times and you will face many disappointments.
- Secondly you will face financial pressures, battles and problems and also a wide range of differences of opinion on lifestyle and how money should be spent.
- Thirdly you will discover that it is sometimes relatively easy to get started on a project, but unbelievably hard to keep it going and at the same time keep the loyalty of the people with whom you are working.
- Fourthly you will discover that roots of bitterness can very easily come into Christian work which, sometimes, due to

Satanic opposition, can be more difficult and complex than in secular work, especially when money and other motivating forces are absent.

This is not intended to be discouraging. There will also be, of course, blessings and joy over breakthroughs in answer to prayer. Missions work can be a lot of fun. Many of the missionaries I know are grace-awakened people who know how to get the most out of their lives. However, keeping a balance between faith goals and unrealistic expectations is part of the process of counting the cost. Edith Schaeffer puts it like this: 'The reality in the life of an evangelist, or a "teller of the truth," is not pointed out as a series of miracles which remove all sickness, hardship, and fatigue from that person, but a series of hard, slogging days of work during which a sufficient amount of the Lord's strength has become evident in the human being's weakness.' (*Affliction*)

This chapter has not been about the huge need for missionaries to go to a large number of places around the world, nor has it been about the tremendous opportunities that exist in missionary work today; these topics are dealt with elsewhere in the book. You do have to be aware of the needs and opportunities throughout the world as you consider your own future, but this chapter has been a challenge to consider seriously your own personal response to the command and the promise of Jesus in the Great Commission. You are called to make a decision.

This decision is not one that you should make on your own. You will need to talk to others about it – family, Christian friends, and mature Christians in your church or fellowship. You will need to become informed about the worldwide situation by reading and getting into contact with mission agencies. Of course you will need to pray and read the Bible as you work to clarify God's plan for your future. (In his book, *The World Christian Starter Kit*, Glenn Myers lists a hundred actions that you can take to help you begin to answer the question, What must I do?) A call to the mission field is not necessarily a feelings-orientated, emotional call, even though some people have those kind of experiences. Usually, it is a basic act of the will as a result of the kinds of processes described in this paragraph. Often it is through a careful process, taking one step at a time. Tetsunao Yamamori in *Penetrating Missions' Final Frontier* says:

From the stories of others who have become involved in mission work, we learn that the initial inner urgings often seem very subtle, hard to discern. In fact, for most of us, the message really doesn't become clear until we act. It is the process of taking action in response to the Holy Spirit's

urging that often provides the real clarity. Without responding, you'll probably never know.

Nor is a call to the mission field a choice
between going or not being involved. Michael
Griffiths, looking back to the early church in his
book, *A Task Unfinished*, points out that, 'The
disciples of Jesus were all disciples, and all were
expected to be equally committed to the
Teacher's cause, and equally concerned to take
the gospel to the ends of the earth.' That is still
true for us now, whatever our particular role in
that great cause might be.

### Suggested reading:

Gaukroger, Stephen, *Why Bother With Mission?*
(IVP).
Sjogren and Stearns, Bill and Amy, *Run With the
Vision* (Bethany House Publishers).
Yamamori, Tetsunao *Penetrating Missions' Final
Frontier* (IVPUS).
Griffiths, Michael, *A Task Unfinished* (Monarch
Books).

### Books referred to:

Tozer, A. W., *The Root of the Righteous* (Christian Pub-
lications)
Lutzer, Irwin, *Failure: The Back Door to Success*
(Moody Press).
Schaeffer, Edith, *Affliction* (Solway).

# THREE

# Taking the Lead

'Leadership is knowing how to get from where we are to where we should be.' (Steve Chalke)

What a huge need there is for people to serve as leaders. If you want evidence of the shortage of potential leaders, look at the painful process through which the United Nations struggled to find a new Secretary General, or the process by which the USA and other countries select the handful of people who are fit and willing to stand for the highest political offices. Most Christian agencies, and especially missionary organizations, are crying out for more leaders, both men and women. I know one mission that has been searching for over two years for a General Director or CEO. There is a need for more Christians to take up leadership, not as an honour or a prize, but as a way of serving the Body of Christ with the gifts and ministries given them. Many, who never expected it, will become leaders, especially in their local church. Being a leader in the home might prove to be the greatest challenge of all.

We need more emphasis in the church on the training of leaders, old and young. I am often reminded that those leaders of the church in Thessalonica, with whom Paul corresponded, were just a few weeks old in the faith. Training can start with the young. I am committed to the task of training people for leadership right where they happen to be, while at the same time presenting them with the truth of a world vision. What a powerhouse the church would be if we could amalgamate the kind of biblical teaching that creates dynamic spiritual leaders in home countries, with the kind of vision which we read about in Acts 1:8. This would lead the church towards a greater forward thrust into world missions. There is a need for leaders who will 'mobilise the people of God for adventurous and imaginative mission'. (Paul Beasley-Murray in *A Call to Excellence*.) May God give them to us.


## Be filled with the Spirit

Much of what I have to say in this chapter concerns the tough reality of being a leader in the church and in mission work today. However, I won't finish without reminding you of

the glorious resources available to leaders in
Christ. Over the years as director of Operation
Mobilisation I have spent much time in the
training of leaders. Sometimes when speaking
at a leaders' conference, I will deal with the
special spiritual and character qualities needed
by leaders in God's work. These are important
and I will write about them later in this chapter.
Sometimes I even get down to the details of how
to make decisions as a leader and how to organ-
ise yourself. This too is important. Most often,
however, I find myself speaking to leaders
about the need for them to work on the basics of
the Christian life – their own spiritual development and walk with God. Nothing is more
important for leaders than this. It follows that in
their relationships with others, leaders must do
everything possible to edify, build up and help
people come more and more into conformity
with Jesus Christ: giving full consideration to
the different circumstances in which people
work in the organisations and movements that
have been raised up by God to work together in
the task of world evangelism.

Most of all, what I want to emphasise when
speaking to leaders is, 'Be filled with the Spirit'
(Eph. 5:18), because it is the Spirit who is the
director of all Christian work. J. Oswald Sanders
in his book, *Spiritual Leadership*, calls his chapter
on the Holy Spirit, 'The Indispensable Require-
ment'. He says that there may be many desirable

qualities for spiritual leaders but only one is indispensable – that they should be Spirit-filled. I am convinced that there needs to be a greater consciousness of the Holy Spirit and His work in believers. Each one must be taught that it is a privilege to know daily the fullness of the Holy Spirit as He exalts the Lord Jesus and is sovereign director of our lives and our affairs. This fullness is not only to do with the emotions and the inner spiritual life, it is also to do with the quiet reality of how we live our lives from day to day (see Gal. 5:22–25) and with the making of plans and the development of strategy in our Christian work. I am especially concerned to say to leaders that we must depend more on the Holy Spirit for directing us as we move forward in mission work. It is so clear from the book of Acts that the Holy Spirit directs missions work.

> But you will receive power when the Holy Spirit comes on you; and you will be my witnesses in Jerusalem, and in all Judea and Samaria, and to the ends of the earth (Acts 1:8).

> While they were worshipping the Lord and fasting, the Holy Spirit said, 'Set apart for me Barnabas and Saul for the work to which I have called them' (Acts 13:2).

The book of Acts also makes it clear that those who lead missions work need to be filled with the Spirit. J. Oswald Sanders says:

It stands clear in the book of Acts that the leaders who significantly influenced the Christian movement were men who were filled with the Holy Spirit. It is recorded of Him who commanded His disciples to tarry in Jerusalem until they were endued with power from on high that He was Himself 'anointed . . . with the Holy Spirit and with power' (10:38). The privileged one hundred and twenty in the upper room were all filled with the Spirit (2:4). Peter was filled with the Spirit when he addressed the Sanhedrin (4:8). Stephen, filled with the Spirit, was able to bear irresistible witness to Christ and to die as a radiant martyr (6:3,5; 7:55). It was in the Spirit's fullness that Paul commenced and exercised his unique ministry (9:17; 13:9). His missionary companion Barnabas was filled with the Spirit (11:24). He would be strangely blind who did not discern in that fact the fundamental criterion and equipment for spiritual leadership. (*Spiritual Leadership*)*

Some people regret the passing of the fervour often associated with an early experience of the fullness of the Holy Spirit, but as it is explained in the book, *Unseen Warfare*, this loss of fervour may be a sign of getting beyond the early stages and of 'growing up'. If you are going to be a

* Taken from: *Spiritual Leadership* by J. Oswald Sanders. Moody Bible Institute of Chicago, Moody Press. Used with permission.

Christian leader you have to grow up. You have to settle into a steady routine of having the Spirit guide you in the daily pursuit of your work and your plans, just as we have seen in the book of Acts. This should be a constant daily filling but not a restless search for new 'experiences'. Many people feel that they need a fresh touch in their lives and they go from conference to conference seeking something new. Of course I am not excluding the possibility of crisis experiences with God, but there needs to be a 'continuing programme for spiritual growth', to quote the subtitle of Ralph Shallis's book, *From Now On*. When God saved you and put the Holy Spirit into your life He put the ball into your court. He may be waiting for you to hit it back. To use another analogy, it may be that God is urging you, as Nehemiah urged the people of Israel, to 'rise and build' (Neh. 2:18).

## Tough realities for leaders

Of course Spirit-filled leadership is not as easy as it looks. Tozer speaks about it in his book, *Leaning Into The Wind*, and this title reminds me of my own disastrous attempt to windsurf. It looked easy, but I didn't manage to stay upright for more than a few minutes at a time. It's not as easy as it looks or sounds. There are many tough realities that anyone involved in mission

leadership or indeed any Christian leadership
has to face up to.

I'm convinced that people of vision, who
want to see something specific happen, must
know how to win the loyalty of others and must
know how to delegate and be a team player. The
bottom line is that we must really believe in
people and learn how to trust, love and affirm
them.

I have learned the hard way how an insensi-
tive word or even the wrong look on one's face
can be hurtful to others and can hinder them in
their walk and ministry. I once spoke to the staff
and crew on the ship, *Doulos*, on the subject of
loyalty and the response was quite encouraging
(that message on cassette tape has gone around
the globe).* I want to share a couple of the main
points.

There are several reasons why building loyalty in mission work is so tough. Firstly, there is
a huge range of very worthy causes which can
distract Christians from the greatest ones. There
is so much to catch people's attention, that
world evangelism has become just one cause
among others. Many Christians are totally
absorbed with the anti-abortion campaign, with
human rights issues or with politics. Of course

---

* OM Tapes available from: Operation Mobilisation,
PO Box 17, Bromley, Kent, England BR1 3JP, e-mail:
www.om.org/tapes.htm, www.georgeverwer.com

I have no argument with people who are concerned with these matters; I am concerned about them myself. But when these things make Christians relegate world evangelism to just one legitimate interest among others and ridicule those for whom it is the main issue, then I begin to worry. In this climate it is possible for some Christians to feel that an emphasis on world evangelism is some kind of extremism and for those on the edge or the outside of the churches to confuse some missions groups with the cults.

Secondly, even among Christians who do have a basic commitment to world evangelism, many are distracted by the extremist books and tapes which circulate suggesting that one particular view is the whole answer to the problems of the Christian life. Sometimes the books are at fault, but sometimes it is the readers who are ready, for their own comfort, to commit themselves to some extreme, grossly oversimplified view of Christian living. This can lead to a damaging form of super-spirituality, which makes people very hard to win because of the strength and narrowness of their views on what is correct. Similar, though less dogmatic, is a kind of false idealism which some people have about the nature of the world of missions, refusing to recognise and finally being deeply shocked by the reality of the weakness, heartache and error which can be present in this type of work. Sometimes of course the opposite can be the problem, with Christians becoming so infected by the spirit of cynicism in the world, that they find it hard to take anyone on trust.

Loyalty normally involves some form of submission and must work both ways. In an age when obedience to parents has been weakened, another difficulty in building loyalty in the task of world evangelism, is that many find taking orders of any kind from a leader very difficult. There is a kind of pride in the defence of supposed liberty. In some cases this can be the leader's fault. I know that I find it very hard to be gentle when giving direction, particularly when I have to work in a second language. There is a need to learn submission without becoming cultic or manipulative. There is also a need to learn how to work with a team of people.

The building of loyalty and teamwork for the cause of world evangelism is a major challenge for leaders today, but there are other tough realities which leaders and potential leaders will have to face up to about the world.

They will have to accept the harsh reality of suffering in the world without minimising it or disguising it with simplistic clichés. Leaders should be able to face up to the reality of a suffering world in which Christians of different ethnic groups are capable of involvement in the massacre of one another. We know that God can bring healing from these things but we must not minimise their impact on people, or pretend that they do not affect us. In his book, *From Tragedy to Triumph*, Frank Retief, a leader within the South African church, has written about the experience of his congregation in coming to terms with the murder of some of their members and the traumatisation of many more when gunmen burst into a church service, opened fire on them and lobbed a hand grenade among the people. He says:

> There is an unspoken feeling among Christians that, if there is to be suffering, it should be bearable and that we should not experience the same horror that unbelievers do. The truth of the matter is that we are often exposed to the same depth of suffering. Our sufferings are not always reasonable. In fact, they sometimes appear to be more than we can bear. Grief and sorrow overwhelm us and we feel as though we are sinking. This is a plain fact of human experience in this world.

Many people have been helped in this area through C. S. Lewis's books, *Mere Christianity* and *The Problem of Pain*. Many have come to know Christ through these books and if we are visionary leaders, we should be distributing such books.

Leaders must also have the courage to face up to the complexities and divisions within the church and on the mission field. The church is divided and this situation isn't going to change very much. Individual churches, organisations or even whole towns may unite, but not the whole church. Even projects that might be expected to unite us, such as AD 2000, are opposed by many and seem to cause disunity. History shows that much of church growth has taken place in the midst of tension and disunity. Let us admit the truth of this situation. Young people especially want this kind of openness from their leaders. There needs to be a greater reality in the church and this will help to break the chains of legalism which are so detrimental to building the kingdom. A naïve view of the degree of unity within the church sometimes results from a failure to appreciate the extreme complexity of the church and the society within which it exists. Operation Mobilisation is a large complex organisation beyond my personal understanding and that is why it is run by a team of leaders, hopefully under the direction of the Holy Spirit. You can be sure there will still be lots of human folly.

Leaders should be able to face up to the power of money, not just in worldly affairs, but in Christian ministry as well. There are many good books about this, but let me just say that a realistic view of wealth and the ability to handle it and make use of it in all its power in the affairs of God's kingdom, is essential for a leader in missions work.

Sexual immorality is an area of great danger for spiritual leaders. Of course everyone is subject to temptation in this area and nobody doubts its power, but I am amazed at how many leaders in the church and missions have had their ministries ruined by sexual immorality. All leaders are targets of the enemy. It is one of his more proven darts and many will face subtle attacks on their minds and perhaps their marriages.

From my earliest years, influenced by Billy Graham's boldness on this subject, I have also spoken out clearly from God's Word on this subject. Again and again we have taken young, potential leaders to verses like II Timothy 2:22, 'Flee the evil desires of youth, and pursue righteousness, faith, love and peace, along with those who call on the Lord out of a pure heart.'

We have been able to distribute millions of books on this subject and thousands have written or testified how they have been helped. Last year, when a book called, *When Good Men Are Tempted*, by Bill Perkins came into my hands, I realised it was spiritual dynamite and we flooded it across the world. We know God is using it. Lois Mowday's book, *The Snare*, is in some ways even more important, especially for people in ministry.

As leaders we must be acutely aware of the frustrations that come from the limitations of our own weaknesses and humanness, as well as those of the people with whom we are working. Sometimes I feel as though I am driving a brand new Mercedes Benz down a German autobahn at 15 miles per hour. As someone who believes in the importance of relationships and the empowering of other people, I have to recognise that I may not be able to go at the speed I want to as a leader. People of passion and purpose have to accept that their own and other people's vulnerability needs to be recognised and taken into account. There may be times when leaders need to move quickly, to be strong and firm with people, but there are other times when we must slow down, pull back and wait upon the Lord and often His people as well. Without this, even at a slow pace, we may end up on the wrong road or off the road in a ditch!

As I have run this marathon race every day for over 44 years, I have especially been amazed by the harshness and yet often the subtleties of pride in its many forms. Even blatant arrogance is not so uncommon among those in leadership. How wonderful it is when people honestly confess this; surely it is one of the doorways to reality and revival. My own struggle in handling criticism reveals things in my own heart which I have not liked having to face. For all of us it will be a life-long battle.

The last harsh reality I want to mention here, for the particular attention of mission leaders, is that of the reality of the lostness of humankind.

The full nature of that lostness may remain a mystery to us, but it must continue to be a major motivator for all those involved in mission work. John Piper, in his wonderful book, *Let the Nations be Glad,* at the end of a chapter in which he closely argues from the Bible for 'the supremacy of Christ as the conscious focus of all saving faith', says:

> So I affirm again that the contemporary abandonment of the universal necessity of hearing the gospel for salvation does indeed cut a nerve in missionary motivation. I say 'a nerve' rather than 'the nerve' because I agree that the universal lostness of man is not the only focus for missionary motivation. Arching over it is the great goal of bringing glory to Christ.*

Let us regularly remind ourselves of John 14:6: 'Jesus said, "I am the way and the truth and the life. No one comes to the Father except through me." '

## Balance in the life of a leader

In the face of all these harsh realities it is difficult to maintain the essential biblical balance which

---

* Taken from: *Let the Nations be Glad* by John Piper. IVP. Used with permission.

is the mark of the Spirit-filled leader. Over the years I have taught much about balance. In one of my old Bibles I have listed thirty pairs of opposites where I have urged the need for balance in the effective Christian life; there are many more. I would like to mention seven areas where balance is of relevance to Christian leaders who are working to fulfil the Great Commission.

1. First is the *balance between faith and common sense*. Often leaders are called upon to demonstrate reckless and daring faith, to take risks. The history of missions is full of stories of leaders such as Amy Carmichael, Hudson Taylor and Jim Elliot. Of course, when the Spirit of God encourages leaders to take great steps of faith, then they have to move, and those who follow them need to try to move with them. But there has to be understanding on the leader's part as well. Leaders need to grasp the fact that they fire others up and pass on their expectations to them. For this reason they need to be aware of their responsibility to maintain realistic aims and perhaps even develop a little common-sense scepticism about what is possible. Young leaders, in particular, need to be clear that the apparent reckless faith of the giants in missions history has often come after years of experience and indeed after many earlier mistakes. I am convinced that many of

the Christian biographies are not totally honest, as they leave out the sins and failures of the great leaders of yesteryear. As A. W. Tozer said:

> In our constant struggle to believe we are likely to overlook the simple fact that a bit of healthy disbelief is sometimes as needful as faith to the welfare of our souls. I go further and say that we would do well to cultivate a reverent scepticism. It will keep us out of a thousand bogs and quagmires where others who lack it sometimes find themselves. It is no sin to doubt something but it may be fatal to believe everything. (*The Root of the Righteous*)

2. The *balance between discipline and liberty*. You may quote Galatians 5:13 to show that we are called to liberty and I would agree with you, but in the same verse, we are also called to serve one another. Where there are rules, there must be some restriction of freedom, but rules are also a way of showing that we want to practise love among ourselves. Another way of looking at a rule is to see it as an exhortation with added strength. After all, grace minus discipline can lead to disgrace. Leaders, with their overview of an area of the Lord's work, may be inclined to overemphasise the importance of rules. An awareness of the strength of the opposing voices of liberalism, in the wider world, may

encourage them to do this. But it may also be
that the pride of a leader is tied up with the way
in which others put his or her decisions and
rules into practice. It may well be that they are
right in what they decide but wrong in their
method of communication and in their attitude
to the people concerned. Those of us with a
strong temperament and strong convictions
often come across in a far more offensive way
than we realize.

3. Closely linked with this is the need for a
*balance between authority and fellowship*. There
are striking stories, from the history of missions, of the powerful authority of mission
leaders. Both William Booth and C. T. Studd
asked members of their own families to leave
the movements they were running because of a
perceived failure to follow the direction of the
leader. I believe that today, as well as the need
for strong leaders, there is also a need for
fellowships to be involved in exercising
authority. In addition to those who make executive decisions, there must be those who
exhort, correct and challenge and there should
be checks and balances against the power of a
strong leader. In many missions organisations
this function is performed by a board of trust-
ees or their equivalent. History and current
events show that God uses a wide range of leadership structures, styles and methods.

4. *Determining priorities* is a constant challenge for leaders. There are so many demands on us that careful use of time is essential. Some of the important balances, which have to be maintained, are between time alone and time with others; between time with family and time with non-family; between work and rest; between work and play; between prayer and Bible study and between witnessing to non-believers and helping believers. Temperament plays a big part in achieving this balance. No two leaders or their jobs are identical. A balance in the use of time needs to be worked out in the context of a particular leader's own situation. People who aren't leaders should also be concerned to see this kind of balance in the life of their leaders and should encourage it by not having unrealistic expectations which put unnecessary pressure on them. Love and teamwork must be emphasized. We will be working on this area for the rest of our lives.

5. Leaders are expected to be *decisive and firm* but there also needs to be a balance between these qualities and those of *gentleness and brokenness*. Brokenness speaks louder than endless work; it cannot be faked. It means taking the sinner's place, admitting wrong, being honest about false motivation and confessing wrong to others. This is not the same thing as failing to take any action because of fear of causing

trouble. Indeed an essential part of the leader's equipment is the ability to stand firm against intimidation. Some people are very gifted at saying things that intimidate others and making them feel inferior. One of the verses that helps us stand against this is 2 Timothy 1:7: 'For God did not give us a spirit of timidity, but a spirit of power, of love and of self-discipline.'

Some people have misunderstood the message of brokenness and have consequently developed an unhealthy understanding of themselves and their own personality – a low sense of their self-worth. Such people will find it hard to be missionary leaders and may even have difficulty in their own country in being effective disciples and missions mobilisers. Leaders will always make waves and need the strength to stand against the intimidation that may result, but they need to do it in combination with a willingness to deal openly, honestly and lovingly with the consequences. For the past 30 years, in our own ministry, we have seen God use the message of David Seamands, especially through his book, *Healing for Damaged Emotions*, which has helped many people in this particular struggle.

6. Balance in the area of *doctrine* is important for the leader. Dr Francis Schaeffer and Dr John Stott have helped me to learn to love purity of

Christian doctrine. A. W. Tozer, and others like him, have taught me to value the daily experience of the presence of God. We need both emphases and they will always be in dynamic tension – a balance between life and doctrine. However, doctrine needs to be distinguished from personal convictions and ideals. Many leaders are in a certain position because of a powerful personal conviction that some particular task needs doing or some point needs making. There is nothing wrong with this, but there is a need to recognise the fine line which separates major doctrines all of us need to believe, and other areas where there is room – or should be – for disagreement. Sadly, many denominations and their leaders are intimidated by interdenominational co-operation because it demands flexibility in their convictions and ideals even though it would not threaten essential Christian doctrine. This kind of attitude is brought about by isolation and can be broken down by bringing people from different backgrounds together to pray and make decisions. Where there are genuine doctrinal differences, then of course these need to be respected. Often, however, there will be opportunities for loving compromise, where personal or organizational principles and ideals are concerned, or at least the chance to agree to disagree, while at the same time pressing on together

7. Finally, leaders need a *balanced view of God*. I love this beautifully balanced view of God that A. W. Tozer gives:

> The fellowship of God is delightful beyond all telling. He communes with his redeemed ones in an easy and uninhibited fellowship that is restful and healing to the soul. He is not sensitive nor selfish nor temperamental. What he is today we shall find him tomorrow and the next day and next year. He is not hard to please though he may be hard to satisfy. He is quick to mark every simple effort to please him. We please him most not by frantically trying to make ourselves good but by throwing ourselves into his arms with all our imperfections and believing that he understands everything and loves us still. (*The Root of the Righteous*).

## A picture of a missions leader

There are many hard words in this chapter and I would like to conclude by giving a picture of the spiritual leader in missions work and by reminding us of the resources available to enable this picture to be developed. It is clear, from what I have already said, that the leader in Christian missions is someone controlled by the Holy Spirit, not just in the emotions and the inner, personal spiritual life, but also in the details of daily life and especially in the matter of missionary strategy. It is someone who is able to build loyalty among the members of the Body of Christ for the task of world evangelism in the face of strongly opposing forces. It is also someone who has the balance of the Spirit in the areas spoken about above.

To complete the picture I want to briefly mention six further qualities. A leader in the world of missions is someone who has:

1. *A vision* – a powerful sense of what needs to be done and the initiative to take hold of it and work towards its completion. J. Oswald Sanders shows how many of the pioneer missionaries were people of powerful vision.

> Carey was seeing the whole world on the map while his fellow preachers were preoccupied with their own little parishes. Henry Martyn saw India, Persia and Arabia – a vision of the Muslim world – while the church at home was engrossed in its petty theological squabbles. Of A.B. Simpson his contemporaries said, 'His life-work seemed to be to push on alone, where his fellows had seen nothing to explore'.

I shall always remember, many years ago, climbing a mountain in Scotland, listening to a tape by Dr John Stott on leadership, in which he pointed out the importance of vision. His great

example was the marvellous story of Wilber-
force; I'll never forget it.

Along with this type of vision goes the:

2. *Sensitivity and understanding* which has regard
for the positions and feelings of the others who
are involved in the fulfilment of the vision,
whether it is something huge, like the 'Acts 13
breakthrough' vision, or something much
smaller, like the sending of a single missionary
by a small church.

A leader should consider and develop an
understanding of their own nature and feelings
and the particular character of their own leadership. There are no simple rules about which
type of person can become a leader. It may not
be clear to begin with who is going to be an
effective leader – some people develop slowly
into the role and may not look like leaders at
first. It isn't only choleric and talkative people
who fill these roles; quiet and reserved people
can be great leaders. Indeed James 1:19 tells us
to be slow to speak. Different character types
are needed for leadership because different
types of leaders are needed: those who pioneer
work and those who consolidate it being just
two of them. An understanding of these matters
will enable a leader to see their role in its broad
context and to understand how it impacts
others. We need to remember the huge range of

leadership types needed in the whole Body of Christ. In one sense, everyone needs some basic leadership skills; this is especially true in the present age of so many single parents.

As leaders, we should be:

3. *People of prayer.* It is hard to put into words how strongly I feel about this. It is so clear in God's Word and most leaders agree and pay at least lip-service to it – but where are those who make this a practical reality in their daily lives? Perhaps the most famous book challenging us on all this is *Power Through Prayer*, by E. M. Bounds.

We should also be:

4. *Encouragers of people.* We should encourage, in others, a high view of the sovereignty of God. We should encourage high standards in the details of everyday Christian life and work: the courage to rebuke in love; to give compliments; to maintain a sense of humour; in the quality of work done; in delegation; in follow-up; in keeping others informed and in being systematic and organised. The bigger an organisation the more complex the challenge.

I have told young leaders that every word of correction must be preceeded by many words of affirmation and encouragement. Even a phone call or letter of encouragement can be a huge blessing to people in the midst of the battle.

As leaders in mission work we need to be:

5. *Committed to high standards in communication*. Much of this will be within the organisation in which we work but, most importantly, we should be communicating the needs of the world to the church. Clear communication on the prohibited subject of money is vital if visions are going to be fulfilled.

I have had struggles writing this chapter because I find it hard to express what is burning in my heart, especially as there are already so many good books on leadership available. Hopefully my final point will get you into some of these books:

A leader needs to be:

6. *A reader*. I hope that you are reading God's Word along with powerful Christian books and that you will go on from there to discover a wide range of books, magazines, tapes, and videos, including some truly great films.

There are a large number of books on leadership and leaders should be using them. However, we should not only be reading Christian books, but a whole range of other books and magazines.

It's a risky road because there is a lot of rubbish out there, but as leaders we must choose this road, there is no other biblical way.

I hope that what I have shared here will whet your appetite to study some of the great books on leadership. Since I began to write this book, *Future Leader*, written by an OM leader, has been published and I urge you to read it, along with the following titles.

### Suggested reading:

Pollard, William C., *Soul of the Firm* (Zondervan).

Thomas, Vivian, *Future Leader* (Paternoster Press).

Sanders, J. Oswald, *Spiritual Leadership* (Moody Press).

Marshall, Tom, *Understanding Leadership* (Sovereign).

Beasley-Murray, Paul, *Dynamic Leadership* (Monarch Books).

Beasley-Murray, Paul *A Call to Excellence* (Hodder and Stoughton).

Bennett, David W., *Leadership Images from the New Testament* (OM Publishing).

Maxwell, Dr. John C., *Developing the Leaders Around You* (Word Publishing).

Maxwell, Dr. John C., *The 21 Indispensable Qualities of a Leader* (Word Publishing).

### Books referred to:

Hodges, H. A., (foreword), *Unseen Warfare* (Mowbray).

Tozer, A. W., *Leaning into the Wind* (OM Publishing)

Tozer, A. W., *The Root of the Righteous* (Christian Publications).

Shallis, Ralph, *From Now On* (OM Publishing).

Retief, Frank, *From Tragedy to Triumph* (Nelson Word Ltd).

Lewis, C. S., *The Problem of Pain* (Fount).

Lewis, C. S., *Mere Christianity* (Fount).

Perkins, Bill, *When Good Men Are Tempted* (Zondervan).

Mowday, Lois, *The Snare* (Alpha).

Piper, John, *Let the Nations be Glad* (IVP).

Seamands, David, *Healing for Damaged Emotions* (Alpha).

Bounds, E. M., *Power Through Prayer* (Moody).

# FOUR

# Being a Missions Mobiliser

A missions mobiliser is a Christian who not only wants to get involved in evangelism and missions work but who wants to *get other people involved* as well. This is in obedience to the Great Commission and to the words in 2 Timothy where it says, 'And the things you have heard me say in the presence of many witnesses entrust to reliable men who will also be qualified to teach others' (2 Tim. 2:2). If we are going to see the world evangelised, we are going to have to see some major steps forward in the mobilisation of the whole church. I believe that every believer should be involved in this great task.

God can use anyone who loves Jesus. My own testimony is that God launched me into missions and mobilisation when I was only sixteen years of age. When I was nineteen God sent me to Mexico. (I actually got involved in raising money for missions, especially Scripture distribution, before my conversion.) This proved to be one of the birthplaces of short-term missions, a movement that has now become accepted by most mission agencies. As we look back over more than four decades, from the earliest beginnings of Operation Mobilisation, we can rejoice over about 100,000 men and women, largely but not exclusively young people, who have been mobilised into missions. In many cases their involvement with OM was only for a summer or a year, but an amazing percentage of those people are now involved in missions or missions mobilisation in a whole range of different ways. Many are back in very ordinary jobs – what I like to think of as 'market place ministry' – but in varying degrees many are attempting to help the cause of world missions. Bob Sjogren and Bill and Amy Stearns put it like this:

> If your heart's cry is for the whole world, if you can't seem to hear God directing you to go to one specific people or area, if you're gifted naturally and spiritually in communicating and encouraging, perhaps your strategic niche is that of a mobiliser. You can encourage, exhort, prod, lure, handhold, cajole and pray whole churches into a sharper vision of their part in God's global purpose.

As I consider these things, I am reminded again and again of the tremendous challenge to go into all the world and preach the gospel to every person. Look again at those verses where the Great Commission is set out: Matthew 28:18–20, Mark 16:15, Luke 24:47,48 and John 20:21–23. Then look again at Acts 1:8 where we have that final statement before the Lord Jesus ascended into heaven, 'But you will receive power when the Holy Spirit comes on you; and you will be my witnesses in Jerusalem, and in all Judea and Samaria, and to the ends of the earth.'

That little phrase, 'The ends of the earth' is one that continues to inspire me deeply. It is because of this that I want to consider six basic principles that need to be taken on board if we are to be effective missions mobilisers as part of our obedience to Christ's command.

## Walking with God

On the opening page of his book concerning the supremacy of God in missions, *Let the Nations be Glad*, John Piper says this:

> If the pursuit of God's glory is not ordered above the pursuit of man's good in the affections of the heart and the priorities of the church, man will not be well served and God will not be duly honored. I am not pleading for a diminishing of missions but for a magnifying of God. When the flame of worship burns with the heat of God's true worth, the light of missions will shine to the most remote peoples on earth.

As with all areas of Christian service, so with missions mobilisation; it is important that we begin by reaffirming that our priorities are knowing God, walking with Jesus and experiencing the continuing reality of His Holy Spirit in our lives. The Holy Spirit is the Chief Executive Officer of world missions. That is so clearly seen in great passages like Acts 13 where the church waited on God in prayer and the Lord, through the church, sent the first missionary team, including Paul and Barnabas, out into the harvest field.

We need a constant work of the Holy Spirit. I often tell the story about D. L. Moody who would emphasise the need to be filled with the Spirit again and again. One day when asked, 'Mr Moody why do you keep saying we have to be filled again and again?' he replied, 'Because I leak.' I think many Christians can relate to that reply. Praise God that He can fill us again and again, just as happened in Acts 4:31, where we read that the believers gathered together in prayer, the place was shaken and they were filled with the Holy Spirit and went out and spoke the word of God with boldness. What a challenge!

As we confirm the importance of our walk with God, as missions mobilisers, so we need to recognise the importance of prayer. Prayer is at the heart of the action and a worldwide prayer movement must run parallel with any kind of worldwide mission movement. Different believers approach prayer with different viewpoints, but without prayer we must acknowledge that missions mobilisation, on the scale needed, is never going to happen. We have clear teaching in Matthew 9:37 and 38, in the very words of our Lord Jesus: 'Then he said to his disciples, "The harvest is plentiful but the workers *are** few. Ask the Lord of the harvest, therefore, to send out workers into *his** harvest field." ' Missions mobilisation, in a sense, starts on our knees – or whatever other posture we may adopt for praying. I actually do some of my praying walking around. Stephen Gaukroger in *Who Cares About Mission?* says:

> We should pray about mission until it becomes a priority! We may not personally be able to take the good news abroad, but we can all pray in such a way that regions abroad are affected . . . Prayer needs no passport, visa or work permit. There is no such thing as a 'closed country' as far as prayer is concerned . . . Much of the history of mission could be written in terms of God moving in response to persistent prayer.

## Taking ownership of world evangelism

Christians must take ownership of world missions. I have noticed a tendency for people to

---

* Author's emphasis

think that some other person or group is going to do it. I notice, in meetings right around the world, that it seems to be only a small number of people who are really taking ownership of the task. To be concerned with missions mobilisation involves a sense of personal responsibility. As we inform ourselves about missions we need also to sense the weight of responsibility to take action. It's even possible to be a missionary and yet not really take ownership of the bigger vision and task.

Taking ownership means prayerfully developing goals and aims. Some have criticised the worldwide AD 2000 Network, with its vision to raise 200,000 new missionaries, for having goals and aims which are too high. Actually, some purely national goals are so huge that if they were all fulfilled, it would go well beyond the 200,000 mark. It may be true of some people that they aim too high, but I think that we have to acknowledge, as Christians, that often our goals and aims are too low. What we need are tasks in which we can see a combination of the 'possible' and the 'impossible'. We want to be filled with faith but we want to be realistic. When we think and pray about the setting of targets, an important scripture is Luke 14 where we are told clearly that we must count the cost of what we set out to do. The more we count the cost of what is involved in mobilising large numbers of missionaries, the more of a 'Mount Everest' the task appears.

As well as individuals, mission agencies and churches will need to have goals and aims in the area of missions mobilisation. There will also often be national goals and aims which may be put together by a national umbrella group in a particular country. It may be done by AD 2000, WEF, Lausanne, DAWN or some other grouping. God has raised up a range of fellowships, structures and institutions and one of the greatest burdens of the AD 2000 Movement is somehow to be able to network together, even though there may be things that we don't fully agree on. As we attempt to do this, there will be times when things get messy. It will be complicated and there will be relational difficulties because agreeing on goals and aims is notoriously difficult.

As we face these difficulties we must decide to put into practice the biblical teaching of 1 Corinthians 13 about patience, love and forgiveness. Biblical unity is essential if we are going to see goals and aims fulfilled. At the same time we can't be unrealistic. We can't spend too much time, effort and money trying to build a kind of artificial unity that doesn't reflect the situation in the real world. There has never been complete unity since Pentecost and it's unlikely to happen now. It is an area where we are going to have to find a balance.

Wisdom and discernment are essential as we consider taking action on missions. A. W. Tozer said that the greatest gift we need in the church today is the gift of discernment. This sometimes comes like a supernatural lightning bolt, but more often it comes as we become saturated with Scripture, as we read widely, as we fellow-ship with a wide range of godly people and as we stay in tune with what's happening in the countries we are concerned about and involved in. I know that in any great area of biblical faith some people can get into extremes. There is certainly the danger of becoming extreme in the field of missions as we set targets and talk about numbers, dates and methods. I am always concerned about these dangers, but I believe that a far bigger problem today is that people over-react to extremism and end up in the deep freeze of tradition, judgementalism, legalism, dead orthodoxy and inaction.

I urge you to develop personal goals and aims in regard to missions and missions mobili-sation. For example, if every person, who had some degree of understanding, wisdom and commitment, had as a target the mobilisation of just ten others, can you imagine what would happen across the world? Often, of course, mis-sions mobilisation will be teamwork rather than the work of one 'lone ranger' who somehow has a special gift to mobilise others. We need small groups around the world, churches around the world and missions committees around the world who are going to spend time in prayer and discussion as they develop definite goals and aims in regard to world evangelism in obedience to the Lord Jesus.

## Developing a greater knowledge of world missions

Closely linked with the development of owner-ship of world missions is the need to improve our knowledge of them. We can do this by read-ing, watching videos and listening to audio cassettes. Then, having absorbed the material, we can be involved in helping others to get hold of it. I believe that we need to increase tenfold the amount of information available on mis-sions and that we must use every method of communication possible if we are to meet the targets that are being set. We need to get people into mission experiences both across the street and across the globe. We need to see that acting *locally* can make an impact *globally*.

In particular we need to gather information on open doors where new workers can enter. There is already an avalanche of information on this but the average person doesn't have it. I recommend that every missions mobiliser be in touch with at least a dozen mission fellowships: getting their information and finding out about the open doors. It takes correspondence, phone calls, faxes and e-mail. When we think of all the communication methods available today, we really don't have an excuse for inaction. Can you imagine the apostle, Paul, having a mobile phone or a computer at his fingertips? God has given these things as tools. We should not be afraid of high tech. It can be misused but this should cause us to be careful that we do use it properly. There are open doors and I believe that as ordinary people and potential recruits hear of these open doors, they are going to respond. First though, they have to possess the information.

We need to appreciate the importance of networking with as many other individuals and groups as possible, often through modern methods of communication, in order to have specific, up-to-date information and prayer requests on the unreached people of the world. The larger groupings such as the 'Adopt a People' movement, AD 2000, Lausanne and WEF can act as centres as we attempt to achieve this worldwide networking. Meanwhile let's not forget the importance of the small mission agencies. There are thousands of these across the world. (Those of us who have decades of experience in missions need to be generous in sharing our experience with these new agencies, helping them to avoid some of the mistakes that we made. This is another reason why I believe networking is so important.) Large groups, small groups and individual missions mobilisers need to be talking to one another.

A further benefit of strong communication links is that they will help to stamp out some of the ignorance that seems to surround world evangelism. Some of the things that I read and even the statistics that I see are just not true. It is amazing what is now on the World Wide Web. Recently, in a huge conference, the total number of 'Christians' in Africa, where there is extensive nominalism in some places, all turned out to be 'born again' due to someone's mistake. People are not doing enough research before they release some of their information. Even stories of great events in evangelism can be shown not to have happened once the research has been done. This produces general unbelief. It causes a lack of trust towards the missions movement and will be one of the most slick tools that Satan will use as we set our targets for the future. We are told in Proverbs 18 and many other places in Scripture that we need to make sure of our information before we open our mouths and speak.

However, we must not be intimidated by these problems because if we are we won't attempt anything. We can still disseminate information but by choosing our words carefully, checking the facts, admitting when we are uncertain and communicating with reality, humility and teachability. That important scripture in Philippians 2:3, which urges us to consider others better than ourselves, is vital in this context. As we contact a wide range of agencies we need to esteem them and take an interest in what they are doing. Let's not be put off by some piece of bad news or some little thing we have read about them and meanwhile fail to see the big picture of how God has used so many different churches, agencies and movements despite their failures, weaknesses and sins.

This will bring us together in a greater way. We can't all work together on a practical level but we can have a good attitude toward other agencies within the Body of Christ. There are many tensions in missions work – some of them are considered elsewhere in this book – and we need to accept the paradox that our unity is going to be in the midst of diversity.

## Using the tools available

There are so many excellent tools available for the task of mobilisation. I am amazed by the amount of exciting material that pours in through my own postbox from churches and missions agencies – videos, audio cassettes, books and leaflets. I have written elsewhere about the need for about a hundred million pieces of missions mobilisation literature. I don't believe that's too much. A lot of this is already being produced by all kinds of churches and agencies. If we can multiply what is already being produced by ten, I believe it would lead to the greatest missions mobilisation movement of all time. This would then enable us to fulfil the phenomenal goals and aims that have been set, such as the ones to reach every person and to plant a church in every people group by the year 2000. As I see it now, it will be many years into the new millennium before this actually happens. We must admit that we are a long way behind.

We can have endless debates about the numbers, the dates and the nature and timing of the opportunities. Personally I think it probably isn't good to fix dates. At the same time our hearts cry out, 'the sooner the better', because we know that these targets are connected with lost people, real people who are going out into eternity without a knowledge of Christ. This is an area where all of us can so easily be involved. Why not invest a few pounds (or a few hundred) in missions mobilisation material that you will be able to take around with you and have handy when the opportunity arises. Use it yourself but distribute it to others so that they can also use it. Have missions parties in your home at which you show a video and share literature. It is unlimited what could happen if Christians realised that they could be involved in missions in a way that will ultimately affect millions of people across the world.

As we see people becoming interested in missions and reading about them, it may be right that the next step is to encourage them to go to some kind of missions event. Almost every major nation is now having missions events and of course individual churches and agencies have them as well. We can get people interested in these events. Let's not be put off because we don't like the music! (How sad it is that the Body of Christ is fighting over styles of music, when history proves so clearly that the Spirit of God has used a wide range of music to bring people into a closer walk with Christ.) Let us not get hung up on areas where we may not agree.

We need to learn how to agree to disagree and get on with the basic living out of the Christian life, mobilising people for missions and presenting the gospel to the whole world. We need to keep one another informed about these missions events however how small they may be. Those of us who lead these events, and who are involved in other ways, need to be sensitive to the wide range of people we are dealing with. Let us not be deliberately controversial. Sometimes purposely being controversial can be a little bit of an ego trip. We get special attention from certain kinds of people and this isn't always healthy. We need to listen to the people who *don't* agree with us and to those who feel we're extreme and that we're stating things that are over-the-top. In this way we can build unity and get on with the top priorities.

Formal education is a powerful tool for missions mobilisation. Most Bible colleges have a fairly good commitment to missions and mission agencies traditionally work closely with them. (My cassette tape, *Why Go to Bible College?* has gone out around the globe). Quite a few Christian colleges (now sometimes called universities) also have a significant missionary thrust; this is mainly a North American phenomenon. In Great Britain the Christian Unions at Universities and Colleges of Higher Education are important in mobilising people for missions. We need an all-encompassing strategy that makes use of all these vehicles for mobilisation. If you consider yourself a missions mobiliser, find out about these places and possibly visit them. Keep informed about what they are doing.

Consider the possibility of going to Bible college for a year or two, perhaps majoring on missions while you get to know the Word of God. However, don't think that the only need on the mission field today is for theologians and sophisticated church planters who are brilliant at learning languages. Again and again we've seen God sending out people with basic skills. We need behind-the-scenes people, mechanics and secretaries, bookkeepers and computer programmers. We desperately need staff who will work in the home offices in their own country. How sad it is that so many people are ignorant about the range of jobs that need to be filled.

The mountain that immediately looms up in front of us (and it happens every time I talk to somebody about the tools needed for missions mobilisation) is, 'Where do we get the money?' The answer lies in a commitment to the kind of intercessory prayer that will release finance for world missions and in a commitment to biblical fund-raising. We need to understand biblical lifestyle and avoid extremes at both ends of the lifestyle spectrum. People need to understand the clear teaching of Jesus about laying up treasure in heaven and that it is more blessed to give than receive. We must think again about the story of the widow's mite. At the same time we need to study history and realise how God has used men and women in the market place who earn considerable resources through hard work and tears and then share those resources with mission agencies and churches for the sake of world evangelism.

Woodrow Kroll puts the case powerfully:

'Behind-the-lines missionaries who finance the spread of the gospel are the most critically needed people in the world today. Tragically, those who are called and trained can't find enough financing to get to the field. They end up doing something

other than what God has called them to do, and
it's not their fault. Their failure is the failure of
behind-the-lines missionaries to do our part.'
(*Home Front Handbook*)

As we develop the right way of thinking and
acting, let us beware of putting down another
agency or another group because we think their
methods of raising money are unspiritual. All of
us, at one time or the other, have been fairly
unspiritual in this context. Whoever is without
fault, let them throw the first stone. God's unity
is certainly in the midst of diversity but meanwhile we need a greater biblical, compassionate
strategy for releasing finance. At the same time,
we need the highest level of reality and integrity
in all our fund-raising.

## Involvement in a local church

Every committed mobiliser should be involved in
a local church. Different people respond to the
challenge of being a missions mobiliser in a
church context in different ways and the response
of their churches is also very varied. It is another
field where we need to avoid generalisations,
judgementalism and, of course, extremism because
Satan is a roaring lion (and subtle at the same
time) seeking whom he may devour in the area of
relationships within churches.

I recently read a book about how a whole church movement became extreme, all under the banner of that beautiful word 'discipleship'. We have new books being published indicating that many people have been hurt in the past 10 or 20 years through extremism in local fellowships and churches. (Those of us in mission agencies know that we also have hurt people when we haven't had enough grace or we have become heavy-handed or dictatorial.) It is not going to be easy, but as we move in the power of the Spirit and take on attitudes of humility, openness and teachability, I believe we can see a new day in regard to our church relationships. This will happen as we work together to mobilise missions and to see that the right percentage of finance goes out from local churches to the regions beyond which are so often only given the scraps off the table.

As we attempt to bring local churches into the missions vision (and of course there are many local churches who are themselves introducing others to the vision), let us use a less threatening approach. Problems can arise where a member is challenged on missions mobilisation outside his or her church and then wishes to introduce the church to the vision. This can happen, for example, when a young person returns from a period of short-term mission work. The book, *Re-entry*, by Peter Jordan, is essential reading at times like this both for the returnee and the church.

Many a young person who was planning a missionary career has been shot down through discouragement, or other fiery darts, during the re-entry period after his or her short term on the field. Peter Jordan has a chapter called 'Horror Stories', which describes and tries to explain some of the negative responses returning missionaries have faced from their churches. We must work to understand this problem and take hold of the kind of reality that is expressed in 1 Corinthians 13, where the practical outcome of Christian love is set out for us.

For many young mobilisers the focus of their activity will be their university. We think, for example, of what God has done at Urbana, through IFES, or through the Christian Unions in the UK. This student movement, as well as Campus Crusade and other movements, is a major contributor to the missionary backbone in the world today. If you are in one of those groups, pray for groups in nearby campuses and be a missions mobiliser.

## Getting others involved in evangelism and ministry

A powerful way to be a missions mobiliser is to get people involved in evangelism where they are. We must not see evangelism at home in opposition to evangelism in other parts of the world. We now have people of unreached groups living among us in most parts of the world. It seems so obvious that people who love Jesus and are committed to world missions will get involved, at least in some way, in reaching out to these people, including students, some of whom come from the most needy nations in the world.

At the same time there is value in getting people out of their own country into another one, both as a learning experience and because it has proved to be a vital part of God's strategy in evangelism and church planting. So talk to the people you are influencing for missions about short-term work. You don't have to have a special call for this. God leads different people in different ways. For some it may be a summer mission, followed by a one or two-year programme, returning then to be a sender rather than a goer. (In the wider sense we are all both goers and senders, or should be.) It is exciting to see how many career missionaries – and we desperately need more of those – are coming out of the short-term movement. Think about using a part of your summer vacation for some kind of missionary activity and encourage others to do the same.

One of the greatest ways to stay on the cutting edge of world missions, is to be involved in evangelism yourself, especially with people from other lands who may live right in your midst. Beware of the struggles you will face as you launch into this: there will be failure; there will be disappointments. But remember that *disappointment* in evangelism can often be God's *appointment* to teach us something greater and something better. We have to stand against the fiery dart of discouragement. I have wrestled with this all my Christian life. God's grace is sufficient. Great biblical, mountain-moving faith does not happen without doubts, struggles and discouragement or even sin. It happens in the midst of those things. When we claim the cleansing of the precious blood of Christ, renew ourselves through the work of the Holy Spirit and come back to the cross, He will enable us to obey His commission to take the gospel to others.

I am sure that God is already using many of you who are reading this chapter more than you realise. Be aware of the subtleties of putting yourself down in an unbiblical way, just as I am sure you would beware of allowing yourself to be puffed up. Be aware that God is doing great things in the world today. He is working through older churches, newer churches, older agencies and newer agencies in an exciting way.

So the answer to 'What's the point of mobilization?' is to release millions of hours of prayer and finances and workers into the harvest force. To see churches planted, discipled, and reaching out into their own cultures – and then on into other cultures. All in order to glorify Him together for eternity. (Bob Sjogren and Bill and Amy Stearns, *Run With the Vision.)*

I hope that you will make a commitment to join this work and be a missions mobiliser.

## *Suggested reading:*

Johnstone, Patrick, *Operation World* (OM Publishing).

Johnstone, Patrick, *The Church is Bigger Than You Think* (Christian Focus Publications).

Johnstone, Jill, *You Can Change the World* (OM Publishing).

Pirolo, Neal, *Serving as Senders* (OM Publishing).

Miller, Steve, *Contemporary Christian Music Debate* (Tyndale House).

Stearns, Amy and Bill, *Catch the Vision 2000* (Bethany House Publishers).

Stearns, Amy and Bill, *Run With the Vision* (Bethany House Publishers).

McQuilken, Robertson, *The Great Omission* (OM Literature).

Trotman, Dawson, *Born to Reproduce* (NavPress).

Kroll, Woodrow, *Home Front Handbook* (BTBUK).

Jordan, Peter, *Re-entry* (YWAM Publications).

Tunnicliffe, Geoff, *101 Ways to Change Your World* (Chariot and Victor Publishing)

Sjogren, Bob, *Unveiled at Last* (YWAM Publications).

**Books referred to:**

Gaukroger, Stephen, *Who Cares About Mission?* (IVP).

# FIVE

# Future Missionaries – From Where?

## Action is for everyone

There are many controversies in the arena of world missions. I mentioned several of these in Chapter One, where I called for a 'grace-awakened' approach to the complex debates taking place concerning the different aspects of missionary work. One of these controversies is so important to the future of missions that I want to devote a chapter to it. It is the debate over whether there is a need for the traditional mission-sending countries of the West, along with Australia and New Zealand, to continue sending missionaries abroad.

The argument for ending this way of doing things is being powerfully stated by several groups and individuals. The case is usually presented as an economic one. It is said to be much more cost-effective to put missions funding from Western countries into the support of indigenous workers, living relatively cheaply in their own societies, than it is to equip and train Westerners with all their expectations of high living standards and needs for cross-cultural preparation. Very large sums of money are quoted in defence of this side of the argument. Some American families are said to need a lot of money, per annum, to stay on the mission field. Single people on short-term work are said to need £16,000. In extreme versions of the argument some single indigenous workers, on the other hand, are quoted as being able to live on £315 a year.

There is, of course, *some* truth in the argument. In Operation Mobilisation, over many years, we have had the opportunity to observe both sides of the debate because we use both methods. We have partnered with local churches in sending out Americans, Canadians and especially British people, as well as others from the so-called First World, while at the same time supporting nationals, especially in countries like India, Pakistan and Bangladesh. I would argue from this experience that there certainly is a continued need for missionaries from Western countries, despite the fact that in a number of places it does seem that the national workers are able to get on with the job at a much lower cost and, in some cases it seems, more effectively. (David Lundy covers this subject in great detail, particularly with regard to OM, in his book, *We Are The World*.)

As with so many of the complex debates going on in the church today, my position is that we need a balanced approach to it; it isn't a case of either / or, but a case of both. More importantly, we need to remind ourselves that ultimately the question of whether to send or not to send is not the most important issue. The issue that should be at the front of our minds as we conduct this debate is, whether as individuals, as churches and as other kinds of groupings, we are walking with God and looking for His guidance as we work to build the kingdom.

The first point to assimilate, in the debate, is the huge size of the task facing the Christian church in taking the gospel to the world. Christians in the 'comfortable' West are often sheltered from the brutal facts and therefore do not live in the light of them. Take for example the population explosion. Consider Mexico City moving towards a population of 25 million; India now has over one 1 billion people and China over 1.3 billion. Consider the population explosion in the Muslim world, such that soon one in six people in the world will be Muslim. Then put alongside these facts the estimated 200,000 Christian missionaries in the world. Not only are the raw numbers daunting, but so is the fact that there are many people groups in the world where there are no, or very few, Christian missionaries. Many of these people groups are in the 10/40 Window*.

The existence of very great need is not in itself an argument for the continued use of Western missionaries. After all, the larger the need, the more important it is to consider how most effectively to meet it. However, Jesus' Great Commission, including the responsibility to take the gospel to the ends of the earth, was to Christians everywhere. As the Lausanne Covenant puts it: 'World evangelisation requires the whole church to take the whole gospel to the whole world.' If this results in cross-cultural complications and large expense then so be it.

## The right people in the right jobs

There are certain parts of the world – South India is a good example – where the nationals can do the job; whether they will or not is another question. There are thousands mobilised in southern and central India and there are thousands of churches in those areas. The same is true in Papua New Guinea, where the need is not for more professional, highly-paid missionaries from outside, but for the mobilisation of

---

* **10/40 Window**. The area of the world between latitudes 10° and 40° north of the equator covering North Africa, Middle East and Asia.

the laypeople, combined with greater spiritual reality and integrity. In some cases, until the missionaries get out of the way, the laypeople will never mobilise. In these cases it is appropriate for the work of evangelism to be taken care of by national Christians and for missionary effort from outside to be concentrated on support, rather than on personnel. The same may well be true of large parts of Brazil, Argentina, Kenya, Nigeria and the Philippines to name but a few places.

At the other extreme, however, there are people groups among whom the church barely exists: the Uighers of western China, the Afghans, the Kurds, the Baluchs and hundreds of others. The argument that the Western church should husband its resources by giving support to local nationals, rather than sending missionaries, is at its weakest with regard to these groups. In many of these places there are no nationals to support. The size, strength and missionary heritage of the traditional sending countries are vital in generating the personnel to go and work in these challenging situations. Between these extremes are countries where there is a significant Christian presence, but where there is still a need for help from outside missionaries from the traditional sending countries, possibly in specialist and training roles.

There are some places where there may be a strong national church which for cultural reasons is not good at reaching out to its neighbours. Bangladesh is an example of this phenomenon. People of a Hindu or animistic tribal background, who account for the majority of Christians in that country, have proved to be ineffective in reaching cross-culturally to their Muslim neighbours, who form the majority group in Bangladesh. Because of this, foreign workers have had a phenomenal impact in Bangladesh and have trained Muslim converts in turn to go and plant churches and win other Muslims. We can rejoice that some thousands of Muslims have gone on for God, largely as a result of the input of foreign Western missionaries. Some Bengalis were involved in the early days; however, these were mainly from Muslim backgrounds.

These examples make it clear that the debate is more complex than simply: 'send missionaries' versus, 'support nationals'. It is, of course, sometimes one, sometimes the other and sometimes both. No matter which method we choose, there will always be plenty of obstacles and problems. We need to accept this, be more honest about them, and then concentrate on ensuring that missionaries sent from the West, go where they are genuinely needed.

I believe that foreign missionaries, going to countries where the church is established, should go in specialist and training roles. I'm not against a dynamic outsider who goes to, say, France as a church planter. I have seen

tremendous international missionary work
going on in France. However, I do feel that our
priorities in such situations should be to help
train men and women to plant churches in their
own country. I have felt quite strongly, for
example, as I have networked with many
church planters in France, that they have stayed
on too long in the particular church they were
planting.

Missionaries, like anyone else, can get
comfortable. When they have a house, and their
children in school, it isn't easy to pull up their
roots. It is also quite hard for people in leadership to say, 'Now is the time for you to move on
to another place and another task and to make
way for the nationals to get on with the job that
you started.' It is possible for pioneer missionaries to become non-pioneering and to find
themselves involved in all kinds of ministry
that could be done by the local believers.

So the false argument that Western missionaries are no longer needed, has been strengthened
by the obvious fact that such missionaries have
not always gone to the places where their
presence was most strategic. My plea is for a
redeployment of staff so that we can give more
attention to the people groups where there are
hardly any missionaries and the places where
missionaries are likely to be particularly effective. We need to face up to the reality that a high
percentage of young people make their decision

about location on very subjective evidence, often basing it on the missionaries they have been in touch with. Since there are not many missionaries returning from the more unreached people groups, there is a lack of influence on young people to get interested in those areas and so a continuing lack of staff.

A missionary who wants a young person to come and work in a particular place because, for example, he or she hasn't been able to raise up a national to do a certain job, can make a location sound like the most unreached place on the planet. But what do we do about the disillusionment and confusion of the young missionary who gets to the place to discover that nationals could have easily done the job, or that someone could have been hired to do the job at one tenth what it costs to send a missionary there? In some cases non-Christian people could have done the job better. We still have a large number of Westerners wanting to go to countries where missionaries are not really needed. The people themselves are desperately needed, but not necessarily in the place where they are expecting to go.

Progress could be made in resolving this problem through careful counselling of young people from the West and through a broad-based training in what missions work is actually about, together with good quality information. Then, for example, when a young person said that they felt they should work in Manila, in the Philippines, because they had seen that there were so many children sleeping in the streets, they could be informed that Manila has more churches than most cities in the world. A more pressing problem in Manila, is how to mobilise the church to reach and care for these children; and then how to finance the large numbers of Filipinos who are wanting to move out as missionaries themselves, but who lack the money because there is nothing left once the church's basic needs have been met. Thank God that good training, counselling and information is available; it needs to be extended to all prospective missionaries.

We must not be extreme on this subject. I believe that the Holy Spirit guides different people in different ways. If you have worked in Brazil and God has given you a phenomenal ministry there, I would probably counsel you to go back to Brazil. Just because Brazil has a huge number of Christians and is expected to be one of the largest missionary sending countries in the next 25 years, does not mean there isn't a place for you as a foreign missionary in Brazil. However, you will have to be different from those who went there 20 years ago. My concern is that often people from the West are not sufficiently flexible to fit into the new missions situations that prevail in places like Brazil and the Philippines.

Why are we using valuable, highly expensive missionary personnel to do jobs that could be done by maybe a non-Christian for a relatively low cost? It is because there has been a misuse of human resources within missions and a low value put on people's time; some missionaries, in whom there has been a huge investment of training and placing, are doing really trivial tasks. This may be all right for the first year when they are in training, learning brokenness and humility, but, in the long term, if people are being paid substantial amounts of money to be out there, they should be truly earning it. Forgive the secular terminology, but if we don't adopt a commitment to excellence in our missionary thrust, I believe that we are going to be laying up big problems for ourselves in the future.

Some churches are beginning to take action over this problem; discouraged by the work that their missionaries are actually doing, they are beginning to ask questions. They are wanting detailed information, from those whom they support, about the nature of the work. They are starting to take ownership. Of course some missionary agencies are reacting against this and so we have yet another controversy connected with missions work.

It is no wonder that the widespread complexity faced in the deployment of Western missionaries, has created the illusion that there is no longer a need for them. In Operation Mobilisation we now have 2,800 workers in 80 different nations. There are huge complexities and problems and I have to admit that mistakes are frequent. People are not always deployed in the most strategic way. I am in no position to set myself up as a judge of other people's methods, but as I cast myself on God, the Holy Spirit has moved me to plead for a more strategically thoughtful approach to the deployment of missions personnel.

## Insensitivity

People who argue that Western missionaries are not needed and that emphasis should be given to the financial support of nationals, tend to stress the cultural insensitivity that has often gone hand in hand with Western missionary activity. This certainly is a matter for concern. In some places there is a great wall between the mission-ary and the local, national church. There are also usually plenty of examples of nationals being in-sensitive to people of other cultures in their own country. Though there may be fault on both sides, it is true that often Western missionaries have taken their cultural and theological bag-gage with them, along with its resulting legalism and grace-killing. We, from the West, often fail by not having a more moderate or simple lifestyle which adjusts to the culture in which we are working. We arrive with a huge number of possessions and all the complexity and confusion which that brings in some cultures. The Lausanne Covenant recognised this problem saying:

> Missions have all too frequently exported with the gospel an alien culture, and churches have sometimes been in bondage to culture rather than to Scripture. Christ's evangelists must humbly seek to empty themselves of all but their personal authenticity in order to become the servants of others, and churches must seek to transform and enrich culture, all for the glory of God.

To some extent this is something which can be faced up to during the selection and training of missionaries. If people have not proved themselves on this front, possibly on some short-term programme, then perhaps they should not be planning to go on the mission field.

This is one of the great advantages of short-term programmes. One of the secrets of OM is that many people are delivered from their 'missionary call' during their time with us! They realise that they are not the kind of person who could be used effectively in tough, cross-cultural missionary situations. This screening process is very valuable.

## Dependency

A great problem created by the emphasis being put on the financial support of nationals by churches in the West, rather than the sending of missionaries, is that of dependency. I learned, very early on, the benefits and disadvantages of this approach. When I first went to Mexico I was still a college student, so the only thing I could do was to get Mexicans mobilised while I supplied the finance, through prayer, for the work they were doing. The first national I worked with, the man after whom we named our first son, left the work 15 or so years later because he found it so difficult to live off American money. He was a Mexican and he didn't want to do that any more. There is often heartache and confusion when large sums of money have to come from one country to support people working 10,000 miles away in another country and another culture.

In our work in India, for example, we are trying to get a higher percentage of the annual budget to come in from India itself; it's very tough. We have to teach biblical fund-raising and we use books like *Friend Raising* and *People Raising*.* These books are needed not just for

---

* Any references taken from *People Raising*, by William Dillon, Moody Bible Institute of Chicago, Moody Press. Used with permission.

foreign missionaries, but for nationals as well. OM is known for its globalisation policy, as we have people from about 80 different countries working in dozens of other countries around the world. However, we do not take people from new, emerging, sending countries unless they can arrange their own support – most of it from their own country and a good part of it from their own church. In the long term we feel that this is the right way forward. The future does not lie in larger and larger sums being channelled from the West to support the work in, so-called, receiving countries.

Sometimes money is channelled in a slightly different way with national Christians being encouraged to go to the West for their education and training. I believe it is less than ideal when we encourage, for example, an African brother or sister to move away from his or her culture and family for five or six months, in order to get further education. It is acceptable in certain circumstances, but I believe it is not the best way. The best way is for these people to get the highest quality education in their own culture or near culture. I have had 40 years' experience of seeing people return from the West, unable to adjust to their own culture. One Christian brother, who studied with me at Moody Bible Institute, went back to India but could not adjust to living there. He returned to the USA, left his missionary call, and has been living there ever since. There are in fact thousands who do not return, or who return briefly and then go back to the West. Let's not make these people feel guilty. If they are going on with Jesus then praise God for that. However, let us be aware of the dangers, for missions work, of training people in this way.

I appreciate the people and movements who are carefully trying to help nationals in their own country to get the job done, by supplying them with books, tools and sometimes finance. However, dependency and paternalism easily come in when we give large sums of money to people to work in their own country. I'm not saying it can't be done, but I am saying that we should count the cost, face the reality of what we are trying to do and avoid making negative generalisations about different approaches. Supporting national evangelists and missionaries can actually help the local church by lifting some of the burden, but it does have a possible downside: the church fails to send.

## The cost argument

The most strident argument in this debate is the one which says that the cost of missionaries from the West is just too great when put against the amount needed to support a national worker *in situ*. I mentioned some of the figures being circulated at the start of the chapter. The whole question of money and the comparisons made between the inexpensive national and the expensive missionary can get greatly distorted and I find some of the things being said rather upsetting because of their inaccuracy.

Many are unwilling to draw attention to the fact that although nationals often live very inexpensively as single people in their own culture, when they get families, the price often seems to go up tremendously, especially if they are interested in sending their children abroad to be educated. I am not criticising them for this, but it but it does make a mockery of the statement that national workers are cheaper. Some of the cheapest people to support on the mission field are Westerners on short-term programmes. There are some exceptions, but in my experience a few thousand pounds can take care of their needs for a year. They can live in dormitories or some form of shared accommodation. On the OM and YWAM ships Christian workers can probably live more cheaply than anywhere in the world; of course they only get a few cubic metres to live in and so not many families can be accepted.

Some of the churches who complain about the high cost of missionaries, need to ask themselves searching questions about how they spend their money. I often find that pastors are receiving a bigger salary than the missionaries being sent out by their churches; they have a house thrown in on top, along with a few other little perks. (This is not always true in smaller churches, where many pastors are receiving hardly enough money to live, and in some cases have to go out and get a job in order to put bread on the table.) It seems silly to me that a church, which has several millionaires and a building programme worth 7 or 8 million, complains that it needs to raise £30,000 ($48,000) for a family to go to work overseas.

The cost of supporting a missionary, of course, varies greatly from one part of the world to another. This further complexity, that supporting a missionary in France is different from supporting one in India, for example, is often not taken into consideration. This adds to the irresponsibility of those who circulate figures like £25 per month to support a local worker. It just is not true. Things are much more complex than this. It may be that £25 from here, £25 from there and a little job on the side could provide enough. However, this can put people with such meagre support under such financial pressure that sometimes they end up being dishonest and unable to handle money in the work of God.

I am convinced that in certain countries some people are gathering up workers, who have no call from God, by paying them a small salary to do Christian work. They simply need a job, there is massive unemployment and so they queue up to get into Christian work. If you have the money you can sign them up. They often don't have enough training and their lives often go out of control. After they get married and have children, there is no longer enough money to support them and resentment, hurt and confusion come in. These are things that we cannot afford in this great task of world evangelism.

It is essential to accept that a large investment is needed for the effective preparation of missionaries. We also need to understand that if we think that supporting nationals is some kind of miracle shortcut toward getting the job done quickly, we will be making a serious mistake. There is no simple, cheap, 'discount' shortcut to world missions, although there are ways in which we can economise and be more diligent. At home or overseas, a more complete picture is needed to deliver us on every side from small-mindedness – whether it's missionary small-mindedness or national church small-mindedness. When most of the money comes from abroad it often leaves the person's local church out of the picture.

We cannot afford the disunity between those who feel they want to put their money into supporting nationals and those who want to be involved in sending missionaries from their own church or country. Not everything can be judged on the basis of money.

> The Great Commission calls us to not only send [money], but ourselves. Just as the Father sent the Son to become man and dwell among us, Jesus sends us into the world to personally identify with those whom we would reach. This will not always be the most economical solution, but it will be the greatest demonstration of love: We cared enough to surrender our comfort and way of life to share God's love with others. (Craig Ott, *Evangelical Missions Quarterly*.)*

Nor must we allow ignorance of the missions situation to cause us to make bad judgements on this issue. A number of Western Christian leaders have a distorted view of missions because they have no experience of them. Sometimes this ignorance can result in false judgements being made about missionaries themselves. Their qualities and performances are judged against the background of the high-pressure cultures that we have created in the West, with all their false standards. Some of these people, outstanding workers on the mission field, are not even allowed to give their testimonies in some of our perfect, 'committed to excellence' Sunday services. I think that this must grieve the Lord of the Harvest, who wants

---

* Taken from: 'Let the Buyer Beware' by Craig Ott. *Evangelical Missions Quarterly* (July 1993), Box 794, Wheaton, IL 60189. Used with permission.

to see the millions who have never heard, receive the gospel of Jesus Christ, just as much as those in the West, spoon-fed as we are with every possible spiritual cocktail and diet.

It is a time for repentance and brokenness, a growth of grace and a turning away from subjective to objective and biblical ways of thinking about how we can get on with responding to the challenge of Acts 1:8. Those of us from the West, whether our emphasis is on the sending of resources for the use of national churches overseas or on the preparation and sending of missionaries, can work together for the fulfilment of the Great Commission which burns to this day in the heart of our Lord Jesus Christ.

### Suggested reading:

Lundy, David, *We Are the World* (OM Publishing),

Taylor, William D., ed., *Too Valuable to Lose* (William Carey Library).

Barnett, Betty, *Friend Raising* (YWAM Literature).

Dillon, William, *People Raising* (Moody Press).

Ott, Craig, *Let the Buyer Beware*, (Evangelical Missions Quarterly, July 1993).

# SIX

# Finance for the Work

## Where will the money come from?

One of the greatest challenges faced by the individual who is led by God to go overseas to the mission field is raising the finance. Traditionally pastors throughout the world are paid salaries. Some larger denominations also pay salaries to their missionaries, especially in the wealthier countries. Most missionaries who go overseas, however, live 'by faith'. I don't really like this term, 'by faith', because it suggests a distinction that should not really apply. In the end, we are *all* supposed to live by faith, trusting God for our needs regardless of the way He supplies. The term is used as a kind of Christian shorthand to describe workers who are not paid a salary in the usual sense, but who rely on God to provide for them, often through churches and individuals giving towards the cost of the work they do. The term 'faith missions' is used to describe missions whose personnel are provided for mainly in this way. Basically, it means raising your own support.

## Raising money

In this chapter I want first of all to look at finance for missions from the standpoint of a person who is thinking of entering this type of work and who intends to live 'by faith', in the sense described above. In the second section I want to say something about giving from the church to the work of missions.

Organisations and individuals vary enormously in their approach to this complex topic of raising money. In his excellent book, *People Raising*, subtitled *A Practical Guide to Raising Support*, William Dillon suggests a spectrum of different methods with George Mueller advocating prayer alone at one end, D.L. Moody proposing prayer, information and solicitation at the other end and Hudson Taylor calling for prayer and information, but no solicitation, in the middle. He then says, 'The question is: which model for support raising does Scripture teach exclusively? Answer: There is no one model. There are many different models and methods.'

As with all complex debates in the church, we need a balanced view that looks at the whole picture of the church's responsibility to build the kingdom of God. This, as Dillon implies, will involve developing a respect for the methods of other groups and individuals. It will involve a sense of gratitude to those who give to the work of the kingdom, whether they give out of their riches or out of their poverty.

Good communication on the topic of money is essential if people are to understand the worldwide picture. We must move away from the attitude which says that it is unspiritual to talk about money. I would plead for a greater understanding of the biblical principles of finance and above all for an attitude which says that, no matter what our 'so-called' fund-raising activities may be and no matter who may sign the cheques, it is ultimately God who provides all our resources and who deserves our gratitude.

One of the main scriptural foundations for teaching on the payment of Christian workers is 1 Corinthians 9:7–14:

Who serves as a soldier at his own expense? Who plants a vineyard and does not eat of its grapes? Who tends a flock and does not drink of the milk? Do I say this merely from a human point of view? Doesn't the law say the same thing? For it is written in the Law of Moses: 'Do not muzzle an ox while it is treading out the grain.' Is it about oxen that God is concerned? Surely he says this for us, doesn't he? Yes, this was written for us, because when the ploughman ploughs and the thresher threshes, they ought to do so in the hope of sharing in the harvest. If we have sown spiritual seed among you, is it too much if we reap a material harvest from you? If others have this right of support from you, shouldn't we have it all the more?

But we did not use this right. On the contrary, we put up with anything rather than hinder the gospel of Christ. Don't you know that those who work in the temple get their food from the temple, and those who serve at the altar share in what is offered on the altar? In the same way, the Lord has commanded that those who preach the gospel should receive their living from the gospel.

The truth of this passage is that the person who is led into overseas missions has been accepted into the work of the kingdom and, because of this, should expect to receive pay, either as a salary in the normal sense, or through the giving of concerned fellow Christians. If you are in God's work you do not have to feel guilty about receiving this pay. You do not even have to feel guilty if people make sacrifices for you to get this pay. You do not need to be obsessed about having a simple lifestyle. As a worker you deserve your wages (Lk. 10:7). You are the ox referred to in the passage from 1 Corinthians and, as Paul points out, God says this for our benefit.

Difficulties arise when people say they are being led into full-time ministry but, for one reason or another, the people in the local church don't accept this person; this often happens when they are not in any discussion, but are just told that this person is going to be a missionary. We have seen for years the interesting phenomenon where people claim to get their guidance directly from God, but then turn around and criticise the church for not coming up with the money. I have known people who claim to walk by faith and not to ask others for money, but who quickly develop a wrong attitude if the church is not enthusiastic and the money not forthcoming. This is all tied in with the need for a higher level of communication and accountability from the earliest stage of a person getting interested in world mission.

Some would say that the problem is not so much the difficulty of accepting money from others as a Christian worker, but of finding that often what is received is barely enough to live on and that sending churches have to be convinced of the value of investing in this kind of work. It should not have to be like this. Churches need to develop a biblical view of money. One of the ways to help them do that, and so improve the situation of those who live by the support of fellow Christians in the churches, is to make certain that they are well informed about the needs.

This communication with the local church is vital. It is the local church who are most important in sending people out and receiving them back. If you have a leaning to missions work, and the church is not already involved, then share it with them and look for their confirmation. You will need to be open and honest with them about your needs, in a loving way which wins their support for the work. There can sometimes be a conspiracy of silence in churches over people's needs. Whoever you are speaking with, your church or other groups and individuals, develop good communication skills to help to overcome this. Some churches actually have more people who want to go than they can support. This can cause disappointment and tension if not handled in a grace-awakened way.

The skills of simply speaking lovingly and effectively with one another, face to face, on the phone and by letter, need to be worked on. This requires a knowledge and understanding of the life context out of which people may be considering giving. Use printed materials to communicate. Think about preparing an introductory letter about yourself. Perhaps you could ask someone, who knows your work, to write something about you. As you develop these skills in raising your own support, think about and communicate the needs of the wider work as well. It is well known that the largest and most faithful financial support comes from personal friends and church family. I believe that many of these people are ready and willing to give cheerfully to support you, but you will need to make certain that each one has the opportunity to do so.

As you communicate your needs, develop your own vision. Without a vision, the work of raising support becomes a drudgery. Remember that the purpose of the work you are entering, is to take the gospel to the lost. This is the vision that guides and inspires me as I work and pray towards financial breakthroughs. The money really is needed. If people can avoid hell by some other method, then we do not need to bother. This reality should cause us to fight for the resources we need and not to be intimidated by the setbacks and discouragement which we are bound to encounter.

Part of having a healthy attitude toward the provision of resources for the individual, is the cultivation of a balance between prayer, taking action and, through it all, trusting God. I can illustrate this general principle with a very painful story. In 1982 Jonathan McRostie, the then European Director of Operation Mobilisation, was involved in a serious car crash which left him paralysed. When we heard about the accident, we mobilised thousands of people to pray about the situation. At the same time, we did absolutely everything we could to get the best medical care for him. A helicopter took him to one of the best hospitals in Europe, for his condition, and there he received treatment from the very best doctors. Finally, however, all we could do was to trust God to care for him. We prayed, we took what action we could and then we left it to God.

In Operation Mobilisation we have often found this balance difficult to establish in the area of finance. In our early days it was policy not to mention financial needs outside the organisation, unless specifically asked, nor to allow young people coming on our programmes to mention their needs or ours directly. We believed that we should rely entirely on intercessory prayer for the mobilisation of finances, while respecting other groups for the methods that they used. I have to confess that sometimes this policy led to feelings of superiority and 'super-spirituality' as we looked at the more direct fund-raising efforts of others. It also caused divisions as some people applied the policy more rigorously than others. It was obvious that information got out about our needs. Visitors to prayer meetings heard about them and many people wrote about them in their personal letters. The gifts of generous people were obviously based on information from within OM. The policy was never intended to say in a simplistic way that we relied 'only on God and not on people', but to many it looked like that.

Some years ago we changed the emphasis of the policy to give greater recognition than perhaps we had in the past to the scriptural teaching that God uses individuals and the church to meet the needs of those who serve Him. Indeed, the New Testament speaks much more about this than 'looking to God alone', in regard to financial needs. Once this was widely recognised, then the need for good quality information, for those who might be involved in giving, became important. We engage in fund-raising and I believe that now our emphasis is more biblical than it used to be, that is: intense intercessory prayer, followed by sensible action and information giving and, behind it all, a reliance on God to provide for us. (Meanwhile we continue to remind ourselves of the need to esteem others in their different approaches to this complex matter.) God can do the impossible but He also works with His people in a day-by-day, sane, wholesome and peaceful way. Hudson Taylor, a person renowned for his prayer and trust of God to provide money, was also an excellent communicator about his work; we need his balanced approach.

It is important to realise that it is not unspiritual, or even worldly, to concentrate our praying on finance. Watchman Nee, in his book, *A Table in the Wilderness*, says:

But when it comes to financial needs, to food, drink and hard cash, the matter is so practical that the reality of our faith is at once put to the test. If we cannot trust God to supply the temporal needs of the work, what is the good of talking about its spiritual needs? We proclaim to others that God is the Living God. Let us prove his livingness in the very practical realm of material things. Nothing will establish in us the confidence in him we shall certainly need to know when those other spiritual demands come.

If we study the parable of the persistent widow, in Luke 18:1–5, we will learn the important lesson of perseverance in prayer. Then, as we pray, we will begin to encounter awkward and difficult situations to test the sincerity of our goals. We must be extremely careful in the area of motives. Do we really have a burden for world evangelism? When we pray for finance, is it with specific God-glorifying goals in mind? God sometimes withholds finance because He is concerned about our wrong view of Him. For example, it is wrong for us to think that we can put God in a box, and attempt to force Him to do what we want. The book of Job teaches us this and shows us the extent to which God will test a person. It is important, while undergoing a test, not to lose sight of our God-given goals. For God does not want to destroy our goals, but to refine us as we move towards them. God may allow us to be tested, by worry about our finances, but worrying will never bring a spiritual breakthrough. If we are unable to win the victory over worry, then I think it is important to talk and pray about it with a fellow Christian.

In John 3:21–22, we clearly see the relationship between obedience and answered prayer. 'Dear friends, if our hearts do not condemn us, we have confidence before God and receive from him anything we ask, because we obey his commands and do what pleases him.' That does not mean, however, that every time there is a lack of finance or prayers are not answered immediately, that a person has been disobedient. This area requires a tremendous sense of balance. Although we must avoid false guilt and the tendency to become too introspective, we must also remember that any sin we commit can be a hindrance to prayer. In the Old Testament we are warned that when an unrighteous person prays, those prayers are an abomination. *Prayer can never be a substitute for obedience*.

Some people react negatively to the pressure that can come with the enormous financial needs of the work they are planning to do. They do not like to be reminded of their need to trust God for such large amounts of money. Nevertheless, I feel that this dependence is one of the greatest realities within missionary work. 75 percent, or more, of the world's population, face one major problem each day – survival. The average, annual income for an individual living in one of the world's poorer nations, is between £400 and £500 per year. Many people have to work 16 hours a day just to survive. In the light of this perhaps we need to keep in mind O. Hallesby's words in his book on prayer: 'Prayer is work'. It may be that some of us prefer to avoid this work.

Along with prayer, there is the need to take action. Some of this action will be the vital communication with churches and individuals that I have already mentioned. At the same time, there is a need to work on your own fitness to receive funding from others. There may be appropriate training that you could do to enhance the value of any money given by Christians for your support. For a young person, two years on a short-term programme may not be enough. Would it be possible to reschedule your time, or make changes to your style of living, so that more could be put into working for funding and increasing the ultimate value of that funding? Many Christian writers speak of the need for Christians from the more affluent countries to modify the way they live in order to take account of world conditions. Paul Borthwick, in *How to be a World Class Christian*, says: 'We can choose to live more simply that others may simply live. There is enough to go around, but sharing our abundance with others will call us to cut back somewhere, to limit ourselves voluntarily, to live a lifestyle that reflects our knowledge of the condition of people in our world.'

He is probably speaking principally here about physical needs, but what he says could be applied equally to the need for resources to get the gospel to those who need it, wherever they may be.

Having prayed and taken action, we must then leave things to God. In saying this, I do not mean that God fills the gaps left between and after our praying and our taking action. As Christians, we know that God is in all these things. Only by His grace is anything achieved through prayer or work. However, there comes a point where we can do no more. We must, without anxiety, allow the Holy Spirit to work in those whom we have contacted, as well as in those whom we have not.

## Giving money

So far, we have been looking at finance from the viewpoint of somebody who intends to enter 'faith' missions work. The other half of the story is the giving by individuals and churches to the work of these people. Scripture teaches us much about finance and giving. Look, for example, at Acts 2:42–47:

They devoted themselves to the apostles' teaching and to the fellowship, to the breaking of bread and to prayer. Everyone was filled with awe, and many wonders and miraculous signs were done by the apostles. All the believers were together and had everything in common. Selling their possessions and goods, they gave to anyone as he had need. Every day they continued to meet together in the temple courts. They broke bread in their homes and ate together with glad and sincere hearts, praising God and enjoying the favour of all the people. And the Lord added to their number daily those who were being saved.

This is a wonderful passage and people emphasise different parts of it depending on their particular point of view. I believe that we should take the whole of it, including the part that says that they sold their possessions in order to fulfil the needs of others. I am not saying that there is a law which says that Christians have to sell their possessions and give away the proceeds. These people didn't do this because of any law, but because they loved people, saw a need and wanted to give.

Sadly, as I travel around the world, I see very little of this passion to give. There are, of course, great exceptions, but often I sense among Christians a willingness to excuse the lack of finance for God's work with easy-sounding clichés. Missionaries having to give up because of lack of money are told, 'God didn't really want you there,' or, 'It was God who froze your finance.' In some contexts, of course, these things may be true, but we need to be very careful before we take a fine-sounding phrase out of one context and use it in another, when it is no more than a feeble excuse for a lack of passion to provide the resources. Sometimes it seems to me that non-Christians have more compassion and zeal to get the resources to needy people than Christians do.

Another important scripture is 2 Corinthians 8:1–7:

> And now, brothers, we want you to know about the grace that God has given the Macedonian churches. Out of the most severe trial, their overflowing joy and their extreme poverty welled up in rich generosity. For I testify that they gave as much as they were able, and even beyond their ability. Entirely on their own, they urgently pleaded with us for the privilege of sharing in this service to the saints. And they did not do as we expected, but they gave themselves first to the Lord and then to us in keeping with God's will. So we urged Titus, since he had earlier made a beginning, to bring also to completion this act of grace on your part. But just as you excel in everything – in faith, in speech, in knowledge, in complete earnestness and in your love for us – see that you also excel in this grace of giving.

God urges us to excel in the grace of giving. Does that sound like the taking of the offering in your church? I am amazed at how low-key the taking of the offering is in many of our churches. Often there is no exhortation or presentation of needs, but just a single, formal sentence. If we are honest about it, we all know that most of the offerings in most of our churches are fairly miserable. There are of course exceptions but, overall, giving among God's people, as the statistics show, is more or less a scandal. Many people do not 'excel in this grace of giving' because they do not know what their money can do. They do not know that a few pence can buy a Gospel of John and that a whole movement, the size of OM, can come out of a single Gospel of John being given to a 16-year-old. Many Christians fail to realise that without their money, things won't happen. They have a feeling that somebody else will take care of it. Some even use the doctrine of God's sovereignty as an excuse for their own materialism or even laziness.

God wants things to happen, but He makes *us* responsible; so it is we who decide whether it happens or not. There are plans to send out 200,000 new missionaries over the next few years (see Chapter 7). This will not happen unless Christians take action on funding the plans. Poor attitudes to giving are accentuated by the fact that we don't, as Christians, talk openly about money. Sex used to be the hush-hush subject among Christians; now it's money. We need to change this and bring the subject fully into the open.

May we grasp more fully why we should have a passion and a grace for giving; why we should learn to release finance through prayer, individually and in groups; and why we should be more honest and open about the subject of money, even though we may risk offending some people. My reason for strongly emphasising these points, which come out of the two scriptures I have quoted, is one that offends some people. It is this: the lack of finance is a major factor in holding up the work of God. Many people are not comfortable with this statement, but I, along with other writers on missions, am convinced of the truth of it. This is what Stephen Gaukroger says:

> As we approach the year 2000 much mission work is in financial crisis. Mission agencies have found themselves making staff redundant, freezing salaries and restricting the development of new projects. Literature remains unprinted; or, if printed, undistributed. Finance for capital expenditure isn't available, so organisations struggle with inadequate premises, out-dated computers and photocopiers, and unreliable vehicles. This makes the organisation expensive to run and relatively inefficient. Yet the resources are available if only God's people would release them.

I estimate that there are about 35,000 young people who have made a commitment to some kind of missionary service. The shocking fact is that probably 95 percent will never make it into that work and one of the main reasons is, that in many cases, we don't even have the money to follow up their initial commitment. We do not have the books and the information packs that will enable them to turn their commitment into action – involving their church, telling their parents and raising the finance.

Surveys in the United States have shown that the process of raising money is a major discouragement for young people entering missions work. They need help with this but in many cases we just cannot give it to them because we do not have the money to follow them up. We should have materials ready for people who make this great decision, anywhere in the world, to tell them what to do next. We spend huge amounts of money in evangelistic follow-up and so we should. We are told that much more is needed for that job and I'm sure it is. But with some notable exceptions, follow-up for mission candidates is neglected. I repeat: *the work of God is held up for lack of funds*.

There isn't enough money to train potential missions candidates. Very few scholarships exist, for example, for people from the Two-Thirds World to do Bible college courses, even though people from the richer countries spend huge sums of money on their own and their children's education.

There is also a tremendous shortage of money for the tools needed by missionaries on the field to do their jobs effectively. They may often need fairly small items – a video player, some books, a bicycle or perhaps a vehicle. I do a lot of flying and I take an interest in planes. I wonder if you know that a *single* jumbo jet costs about £300 million! Why do Christians have to specialise in being small-minded about supplying the tools which people need to do their job?

Since the Lausanne Conference in 1974, there has been a greater emphasis among missions on holistic ministry – providing for people's physical and other needs as well as taking the gospel to them. Many missionaries were dismayed by this extra burden placed on them while struggling with limited resources to do the basic job. If the church is concerned to achieve the balance between meeting people's spiritual needs and their other needs then the huge cost of doing so must be accepted. This work too is held up through the lack of funds.

Mobilising the church to raise up missionaries and to pray for mission work takes money. The materials and the communication methods needed to keep Christians informed of the worldwide situation, so that they can pray and take action, are expensive. We are told that modern communication methods such as e-mail are cheap; e-mail certainly is cheap once you have bought your modem, trained people to use it and employed someone to supervise the network. It all needs funding. I estimate that we have about 10 per cent of what we need to mobilise the church to pray and take action on missions. Yes, even the church's capacity to pray effectively and plan for action is held up through the lack of funds.

I have written in this chapter about the need for those planning to go into mission and ministry to be proactive in their approach to raising their finances and to expect to be funded willingly and cheerfully by individuals and churches, without guilt and with a sense that, as labourers in God's work, they are worthy of their wages. If this is to happen, for all of the people who make a decision to enter this type of work, then there will have to be a change of mind in the church. Many people reading this will already be giving to missions and many will be unable to give more. My aim is not to make you feel guilty, but my plea is for a vision throughout the church of what money could achieve if it was available for missions work. Let us seek God together, learning from His word and from each other, so that as we grow in faith and obedience in this area, we may see finance released to meet our own legitimate needs and to enable the gospel to reach out to the ends of the earth.

**Suggested reading:**

Maiden, Peter, *Take My Plastic* (OM Publishing).
Hallesby, O., *Prayer* (IVP).
Hilton, Ted, *Building a Support Team* (OM Canada).

**Books referred to:**

Borthwick, Paul, *How to be a World-Class Christian* (Victor Books).

**Suggested tapes:**

Verwer, George, *Does The Lack of Funds Hinder God's Work? Fund Raising is Team Work.*

# SEVEN

# Acts 13 Breakthrough

## The need for 200,000 new missionaries for a new millennium

Never, in the history of the church, have there been so many special programmes and campaigns around the world. The highest goals and aims are being set today by a range of denominations and agencies. Many of these organisations have been tied together in the 'AD 2000 and Beyond' movement. The goal of this movement is that everyone in the world should receive the gospel and that the church should be planted in every people group. One track of this movement is responsible for encouraging and coordinating the mobilisation of 200,000 new missionaries by the year 2000. It is this vision which has been given the name 'Acts 13 Breakthrough' in response to the example of the Antioch church in Acts 13:2, who obeyed God's leading to ' "Set apart for me

Barnabas and Saul for the work to which I have called them." '

As chairman of this particular track, I have often felt discouraged by a sense of the impossibility of mobilising this number of new workers. At times, the aims of some of the people and groups involved seem not only unrealistic, but ridiculous, and in some cases not in line with what the Bible teaches. However, I am convinced, that in the debate about the setting of targets, there are more arguments in favour than against. I am committed to work with those who love the Lord Jesus to build on the teaching of the Word of God to achieve these aims. For all the debating, one thing is certain: the goals and visions of this and other movements will never become a reality without the massive mobilisation and education of millions of believers.

As I have grappled with my own and other people's doubts about this movement, I have sensed a renewal in my own life and vision. God has rebuked me for my doubts. On a flight from Cordoba to Buenos Aires, in 1996, God met me and began to pour thoughts into my mind as to how the goal could be achieved.

Before we look at the detail of how and from where 200,000 missionaries could be raised up, let us think about the world situation and the character of the mission effort in the Body of Christ which make it necessary to even consider raising this number of new workers.

One of the most compelling reasons for wanting to mobilise this great number of new missionaries is the size of the task of world evangelism. There are now about as many people in India alone, as there were in the entire world when William Carey, the great missionary to India, launched out in 1793. There are statistics which show clearly that the Christian church is growing proportionately more quickly than the world population. This of course is tremendous news, but with world numbers moving towards the staggering figure of 6 billion people, how do we begin to calculate the number of Christian workers needed to reach them? I don't think that the average Christian, especially in Western countries, is able to answer this question because they do not have a good understanding of the population explosion.

## Who will do this job?

When we think about the task of reaching these huge numbers, we may visualise the job being done by, what we think of as, 'traditional' missionaries – people with full-time, lifelong careers on the field, witnessing for Christ, teaching the Bible and planting churches among hitherto unreached people groups. Of course, there are missionaries like this, but in many ways this is a false picture, which can distort our view of the number of workers who are needed to take the gospel to the whole world. We may need to adjust our view of how missionary work is being done. We can look at this in four areas.

*Firstly*, there is a very high return rate of missionaries from the field. There are many reasons why missionaries may return early, including illness and the desire to take up posts in home offices. I wonder whether lack of adequate training may also sometimes bring missionaries home early. Once home, they may continue to work, but someone is needed to take their place on the mission field. This point is brought home forcefully by the statistic which says that the average term for a career missionary on the field is *ten* years. In the light of this, we may need to revise our impression of the 'traditional' missionary career and what it can achieve.

*Secondly*, many who go to the mission field are going into some form of work which is not directly evangelistic – sometimes known as 'tentmaking'. There are two categories of 'tentmakers'. Firstly there are the people who have gone specifically to share their faith and build the kingdom. They are trained for a specialism and prepared for the country, and while most of their time will be spent doing their job, the principal motivation for being there will be to win people to Jesus Christ.

Secondly, there are the tentmakers who, by God's providence, go to another culture because employment takes them there. Many Indians, Koreans, Filipinos, Americans, British and others are scattered around the world because they need a job. Many are happy to be in their own church but are hesitant to reach out cross-culturally. However, if they should make a commitment to evangelism and missions, then, overnight, they shift from potential missionary to actual missionary. Knowledge of the language may make them especially useful. I am not aware of any statistics which could tell us the size of this potential missionary force. However vital these two categories of tentmakers may be, they are not full-time workers in evangelism, Bible teaching and church planting. We count them as missionaries, which indeed they are. But as we estimate the numbers needed to achieve some of the ambitious aims being set by the church, we must be careful to distinguish between the different types of work missionaries do.

In launching visions such as 'AD 2000 and Beyond' we are not trying to manipulate the type of work which churches send their missionaries to do. Of course the 'so-called' back-up people in missions are absolutely vital. Can you imagine how many excellent administrators, mechanics or computer programmers it takes to run a worldwide mission thrust? These people will all continue to be needed. Each one of us, in our different organisations and in our different denominations, will have our particular focus and vision. However, when we think about the number of people we want to send out to witness, to teach the Bible and plant churches, we will also need to think about these other great numbers of people needed to back them up.

The 200,000 will include large numbers of older people. Many of them are well suited to tentmaking ministries and also behind-the-scene tasks. People are taking early retirement and some are self-supporting, which is a huge help. Society no longer talks of one career but two, three or even four. Even at the age of seventy, many are taking on new careers. There is an enormous potential for workers among this sector of society. They may take over positions in home offices, releasing younger people to go out and learn new languages. It's hard to learn a new language once you are into your fifties – though no doubt some people will disprove this. We hope that these 200,000 missionaries will include many tentmakers and so it will be hard to measure precisely all that the Holy Spirit is doing. There are going to be a lot of workers out there, in response to prayer, who will not appear in the statistics, but when we get to heaven we'll find out that they were part of the

AD 2000 movement – or something else that came before, or after it.

*Thirdly*, in the same way that many missionaries go to do work which is behind the scenes, or to do tentmaking, many go to parts of the world where the church already exists and not to unreached people groups. *Missionary Monthly*, of March 1996, says:

> Possibly 80% of all missionaries are being sent to areas of the world where the church already is planted – the urgent need is for a majority of new missionaries to be sent to areas where the gospel has not yet been preached, at least where the need is greater than where the church already exists. Each local congregation can help to redirect missionary resources by setting the goal of helping to send and support missionaries assigned to pioneer areas of the world. Some may be sent as tentmakers obtaining technical or professional employment in closed countries as a means of personal witness.

*Fourthly*, the way in which an over-simplified, traditional view of what missionaries do can distort our thinking about the numbers needed, is in the area of holistic ministry, which was mentioned in the last chapter. We are not, after all, just winning people for Jesus and planting churches, but we are trying to build the kingdom of God among every people in the world.

Some people see this as a new approach. It's actually not new in many mission agencies. It certainly isn't new to the Salvation Army for example. Many evangelicals were not very much involved with this approach before the great Lausanne Congress of 1974. The Lausanne Covenant, which resulted from that Congress, says: 'Although reconciliation with man is not reconciliation with God, nor is social action evangelism, nor is political liberation salvation, nevertheless we affirm that evangelism and socio-political involvement are both part of our Christian duty. For both are necessary expressions of our doctrines of God and man, our love for our neighbour and our obedience to Jesus Christ.'

Through the influence of many men and women, including a good number from Latin America, it has been agreed upon by a high percentage of missionary leaders, that we must be more holistic in our approach, combining social concern with basic evangelism. Of course, the moment we say this, we need to start counting the cost, because if this is to be our approach, we need far more workers. I think of Youth with a Mission who focused on a holistic, social concern ministry in Amsterdam. At one point they must have had more than 300 people just in Amsterdam – one city that already has many churches. Statistics show that a quarter of European and North American cross-cultural missionaries are currently engaged in translation, evangelisation, church planting, and teaching. Three-quarters are assigned to administration and support work (mentioned above) and to ministries in areas such as agriculture, aviation, community development, literacy, medicine and relief efforts. Surveys have shown that it is hard for the average missionary to get much time to present the gospel to non-Christians.

This is an important issue for us to face up to. How many of us realise how many staff it takes to run one hospital; how many people it takes to have a children's rescue programme in a major city in Brazil; how many people it takes to run an AIDS hospice; how many to staff a radio station or a TV station; and how many to staff a publishing house in countries such as Bulgaria or Mongolia or some other new mission field where literature is desperately needed? What about staffing the schools, the training institutions and the Bible colleges all over the world? What about all the other tasks that are basic to a full-scale, holistic missionary thrust? All these questions should make us think about numbers in a new way. When we make our ambitious statements about all the things we want to do to meet people's physical and other needs, we must start to put up the workers and the money to make this happen. We must start to get our churches into a paradigm shift so that they will understand that a lot of these ambitions will be just *statements* if we don't get the people needed.

## How can it be done?

I have said that there are four ways that we might tend to underestimate the numbers needed to fulfil the goals which are being set and that these need to be seen in the context of an explosion of world population. Some of us will also have to shift our thinking about some of the *methods* by which the goals will be achieved. Today, almost every nation – though not every people – is both sending and receiving missionaries. This radical change has affected Operation Mobilisation. For example, 20 years ago, Great Britain was mainly a sending country; today it is also a major receiving mission field within OM. Many other missions are facing the same challenge. We need to understand that regardless of what we say, or even what great missionary leaders may say, this change is happening, whether we like it or not.

Perhaps we don't think large numbers of Brazilians should come to evangelise Britain; in one sense it doesn't matter what we think because they're going to come anyway. There

will be people from Papua New Guinea who
come to help evangelise Europe. The Japanese
already send missionaries to many different
parts of the world, even though the Japanese
church is always described as being so small; it
may be small but it is obviously quite healthy
in certain places and it has been sending
missionaries to Bangladesh, for example, for
some time. The Lausanne Covenant foresaw
this change nearly 25 years ago when it said
this: 'Missionaries should flow ever more
freely from and to all six continents in a spirit
of humble service. The goal should be, by all
available means and at the earliest possible
time, that every person will have the opportunity to hear, understand, and receive the good
news.'

So, as we try to plan this aspect of the vision,
with all its complexity, we don't want to get into
controversy on details about who does what
and who goes where. We can try to influence
people constructively on those matters, but the
details of the vision will only be realised when
major denominations and major church movements take ownership of it. In the field of
missions we are living in a very different world
from that of 20 years ago. It is important to
understand that when we pray about 200,000
people, we're not talking about just traditional
missionaries from the Western countries. If we
are honest in recognising what the Spirit of God

is doing now, then we are talking about people coming from *every* part of the world and going to *every* part of the world, as the Lausanne Covenant suggested. When we realise this, perhaps the goal of 200,000 is not so wild after all.

Of course, it's possible to become too concerned with numbers of people sent out; to assume that the goal can be achieved by such and such a number of missionaries from this place travelling to work in that place. Keep in mind that our first burden is not to concentrate on numbers, but to complete the task – to obey the Lord. My view is that world evangelisation is not tied only to missionaries, but to the church and to church growth. Once a missionary plants a church, then that church becomes equally important in any ongoing work in that place. It is the dynamic combination of missionary work and church growth together that is going to bring the breakthrough. Let me give two examples. If the churches in Uttar Pradesh, India, catch a vision for the Muslims around them, then perhaps a relatively small number of missionaries either from abroad or other parts of India would be needed for evangelism and church planting. So far this has not happened to any great degree and so thousands of missionaries from outside could easily be used in Uttar Pradesh where there are over 150 million people of whom over 19 per cent are Muslims.

The same is true in Turkey, which could absorb several thousand more missionaries and not see the job done. However, if there is a breakthrough and if, as a result of prayer and the 300 or 400 workers, who are there now, Turks start coming to know Jesus, and Turkish churches start to be established, then they will be able to complete the pioneer missionary work themselves, without the need for further large numbers of outside missionaries. It isn't the sheer number of foreign missionaries that is important. It is true that church planting in some of these countries that are so big – 70 million people in Turkey – is going to take a significant number of people. However, I am convinced that if we have even one eighth of the 200,000, suddenly in the next few years, moving into the 10/40 window then, subject to seeing breakthroughs in answer to prayer, we could fulfil the goals that we believe God has given us. Meanwhile, it is my conviction that unless a much higher percentage of biblical churches throughout the world get involved in missions and evangelism, the task will not be done, even by 200,000 new missionaries.

Church multiplication is going on in many countries of the world. Through the impact of the amazing DAWN movement (Discipling Whole Nations) and others, whole denominations have started to plan for growth and multiplication. Some of us would consider this to be a fairly normal thing, but many denominations have not been in that mode of thinking, especially that of multiplying churches. My questions, especially to any who are involved in church multiplication, are these: Why can't we multiply churches that are in the Acts 13 paradigm?

Why can't we multiply churches who will immediately begin thinking seriously about missions even if they are small, even if they are new? After all, the Antioch church was small and new. If we could, this would mean that all these new churches would at least be working towards sending their Paul and Barnabas as soon as possible. This could bring a complete revolution to the mission scene. At the moment so many small churches, especially in the Two-Thirds World, don't feel they can do this. They may not have the money; they may be having trouble paying their pastor; they don't feel they are mature enough or that they have been established long enough. After a couple of years many of them are already into a bare-survival syndrome; the thought of sending out a missionary is beyond them. Despite this, many Christian leaders in Two-Thirds World countries have grasped this Acts 13 vision. They see that it can get even a small local church, possibly in partnership with another, to say that it is possible to send out at least one missionary.

How can Christians in places like the UK, USA, Canada and other more wealthy lands, with hundreds of thousands of people in ministry, think that 200,000 for the rest of the world is too high a number or that they are not needed? It is a paradox that we need to search our hearts about. There are churches, who have a staff of up to 50 paid people, who are not sending out career missionaries to places in the world where the church does not exist and where the scriptures have not been distributed. It will perhaps be hard for some people to face up to the reality of this.

There are some model churches who have faced this reality and are attempting to find a degree of balance between what they put into their own local ministry and what they give to the rest of the world. However, it seems that an unbalanced view of money is playing too big a role in the thinking of some Christian leaders and organisations. Some phenomenal salaries are being paid to people, especially those in executive positions, and to the senior pastors of huge churches. It is no surprise then that the word is out that American missionaries cost too much. This in turn has given birth to other negative generalisations about American missionaries. Some churches in the West have decided not to send missionaries from their own church because they consider it cheaper to support nationals. False information about what it costs to support nationals has brought much confusion and hurt in the work of God in many places.

Only a tiny percentage of the Lord's people's money is going into cross-cultural missions. If we really believe that the gospel is for everyone, then surely the situation must change. Every believer and church must be ready to give, passionately and cheerfully, a higher percentage of all money for world missions and especially for the cause of reaching the unreached. Evangelical leaders too should speak out more boldly about the need for missionaries to go out into the harvest field.

## The numbers

I began this chapter by explaining how God had encouraged me on a flight from Cordoba to Buenos Aires; how He had turned me around from the discouragement I was feeling about the huge number of people who needed to be raised up in order for the vision of 'Acts 13 Breakthrough' to be realised. How could 200,000 people be raised up? Where would they come from?

I began to understand that one way to stop the figure, 200,000, seeming too daunting, was to break it down into its component parts. TABLE 1 does this for us. It shows how many new workers each church of a certain size would need to send. The key word from Acts 13 is 'church'. It is the church who should send the workers and there are now over a million churches in the world. There is, of course, a debate in the church about whether individual churches *themselves* should send missionaries or whether they should always rely on the expertise of a mission agency. I don't want to write about that debate at this point. As is so often the case it seems likely that a balance between the two is what is needed. The point that I am making here is a more fundamental one. It is expressed well by Bob Sjogren and Bill and Amy Stearns in a chapter that deals with this debate in *Run with the Vision*. They say, 'Regardless of the options – agencies alone sending missionaries, a local church sending missionaries, or a realistic partnership in sending – involvement on the field is crucial to a local church's vision of God's heart for the whole world.'

TABLE 1 shows how the numbers goal could be fulfilled if just 100,000 churches were to get involved in this way.

Table 1 *Numbers of Churches Needed to send 200,000 New Missionaries (According to Country and Area)*
(This represents less than 10% of the churches in the world)

| | |
|---|---|
| Australia | 2,000 |
| Canada | 5,000 |
| Caribbean | 1,000 |
| Central America & Mexico | 5,000 |
| Eastern Europe | 5,000 |
| East Asia Pacific | 4,000 |
| Great Britain | 5,000 |
| Korea | 5,000 |
| New Zealand | 1,000 |
| Rest of Africa | 6,000 |
| Scandinavia & Finland | 1,200 |
| South Africa | 4,000 |
| South America | 10,000 |
| South Asia (this includes India, Pakistan, Nepal & Sri Lanka) | 15,000 |
| USA | 25,000 |
| Western Europe | 4,800 |
| Rest of the World | 1,000 |
| Total | 100,000 |

TABLE 1 needs to be looked at in conjunction with TABLE 2 which gives guideline numbers for churches of different sizes. These are only guidelines and could only be achieved if churches were to take ownership of this whole vision. Churches would need to hold meetings specifically to answer the question: How many new workers are we planning to send in the next few years?

Table 2

| Churches over (number of people) | Send |
|---|---:|
| 10,000 | 20 |
| 5,000 | 10 |
| 2,000 | 5 |
| 1,000 | 4 |
| 500 | 2 |
| Under 500 | 1 |

It is also useful to break the numbers down into the parts of the world they might come from. TABLE 3 gives this information. We can't dictate where God is going to choose to *send* these people, but we know that, the way things are going, they will be *coming* from every nation in the world where the church exists.

Table 3 *Breakdown of numbers of churches from different areas*

| Western Europe | |
|---|---:|
| Ireland | 100 |
| Belgium | 100 |
| France | 150 |
| Spain | 150 |
| Portugal | 100 |
| Italy | 100 |
| Greece | 50 |
| Austria | 50 |
| Switzerland | 1,000 |
| Germany | 2,000 |
| Netherlands | 1,000 |
| | 4,800 |

Table 3 (*continued*)

| | |
|---|---:|
| **Scandinavia** | |
| Norway | 500 |
| Denmark | 100 |
| Sweden | 300 |
| Finland | 300 |
| | 1,200 |
| **Eastern Europe** | |
| Poland | 500 |
| Czech Rep. | 100 |
| Slovakia | 100 |
| Hungary | 350 |
| Romania | 200 |
| Bulgaria | 50 |
| Ukraine | 300 |
| Albania | 100 |
| Latvia | 50 |
| Belarus | 30 |
| Estonia | 55 |
| Lithuania | 50 |
| Croatia | 30 |
| Slovenia | 30 |
| Serbia | 55 |
| Russia | 3,000 |
| | 5,000 |
| **Central America** | |
| Guatemala | 1,000 |
| Nicaragua | 350 |
| Panama | 200 |
| El Salvador | 400 |

Table 3 (*continued*)

**Central America** (*continued*)

| | |
|---|---:|
| Costa Rica | 1,000 |
| Mexico | 2,000 |
| Belize | 50 |
| | 5,000 |

**South America**

| | |
|---|---:|
| Argentina | 1,250 |
| Bolivia | 500 |
| Chile | 1,000 |
| Peru | 250 |
| Ecuador | 250 |
| Paraguay | 250 |
| Uruguay | 250 |
| Colombia | 500 |
| Venezuela | 500 |
| Guyana | 100 |
| Suriname | 100 |
| Fr. Guiana | 50 |
| Brazil | 5,000 |
| | 10,000 |

**Africa**

| | |
|---|---:|
| Angola | 100 |
| Cameroon | 100 |
| Egypt | 200 |
| Ethiopia | 500 |
| Ghana | 500 |
| Kenya | 500 |
| Madagascar | 100 |
| Malawi | 100 |

Table 3 (*continued*)

**Africa** (*continued*)

| | |
|---|---:|
| Mozambique | 100 |
| Nigeria | 2,000 |
| Rwanda | 100 |
| South Africa | 4,000 |
| Sudan | 200 |
| Tanzania | 500 |
| Uganda | 200 |
| Zaire | 300 |
| Zambia | 100 |
| Zimbabwe | 100 |
| Rest of Africa | 300 |
| | 10,000 |

**East Asia**

| | |
|---|---:|
| Philippines | 1,000 |
| Indonesia | 500 |
| Malaysia | 500 |
| Singapore | 500 |
| Hong Kong | 500 |
| Japan | 200 |
| Thailand | 100 |
| Burma | 100 |
| Taiwan | 50 |
| Rest of E. Asia | 550 |
| | 4,000 |

**Australasia**

| | |
|---|---:|
| Australia | 2,000 |
| New Zealand | 1,000 |
| Papua New Guinea | 200 |
| Pacific Islands | 100 |
| | 3,300 |

The figures in these tables may look like hopeful guesses to some; it is true that the reality will be a thousand times more complex than any table of figures can show. However, they are not as daunting as they may look. For example in TABLE 1, out of the very big churches, we are looking for 200 to send 20 new workers. There are thousands of these very big churches in the world and some have already done this. What we are looking for is an escalation of a process already under way. At the lower end of TABLE 1, it suggests that fifty thousand churches could send one new missionary. This sounds like a lot of small churches, but there are at least a couple million of them and a significant number are already sending workers.

## Numbers aren't everything

Breaking the numbers down in this way gives us something concrete to aim for. However, don't get hung up on numbers. Get your church and your denomination involved. They will contextualise this vision into their own situation, and get God's guidance as to what they should do and what numbers should be involved. Let us especially bring the whole matter into the heart of our prayer ministry. In Matthew 9, we are commanded by the Lord Himself to pray that the Lord of the harvest will send out workers into the harvest field. If you choose to pray for *more* than 200,000 new cross-cultural workers – praise the Lord! Have mercy on those of us who are concentrating on this smaller number that is still considered quite wild by a number of members of the Body of Christ.

It is important to remember that the 'Acts 13 Breakthrough' vision will only be fruitful if it is pursued in harmony with all kinds of other strategies, visions and godly principles that God has been using throughout the life of the church. Let me mention a few of these that must go hand in hand with the goal of raising large numbers of new workers and with taking the gospel to all peoples.

*Firstly*, we need a greater renewal and reality in the churches. By this I mean Christians moving on from a superficial walk with God to one which accepts the challenges which God is putting before us today. I also mean an honest and open attempt to break down barriers between different visions and different emphases in the church and working for a Holy Spirit marriage of them.

*Secondly*, it is so important that there should be a 'grace awakening'. By this I mean a renewed emphasis on the kind of love which 1 Corinthians speaks about. I believe that unless we have more of that big-heartedness towards one another – individuals and organisations –

our grand visions for large numbers of new workers will not become a reality. We need *every* member of the Body of Christ.

*Thirdly*, a greater discipline is needed in prayer, in studying the Word of God and in giving. These basic, godly activities cannot be separated from other visions that God has given us.

*Finally*, we must beware of allowing negative thinking to kill our creativity or vision. The history of the church shows that often God is working in the midst of what looks, to us, like a mess. Often what we think is a casualty, is not a casualty with God. 43 years of ministry across the globe and involvement with thousands of people, has confirmed my view that while we must work for the highest standards of profes- sionalism in all we do, God often achieves tremendous things through the most unlikely people, organisations and situations. Let us not expect that the raising up, by the church, of 200,000 new missionaries will be a neat and tidy process.

# Tapes Available

Contact George Verwer's website for information
and details of how to purchase copies of his tapes

**www.georgeverwer.com**

# The George Verwer Collection

*ISBN 1-85078-296-2*

George Verwer has inspired and encouraged thousands in their Christian discipleship. Now three of his best-loved books, *The Revolution of Love, No Turning Back*, and *Hunger For Reality* are brought together in this three in-one collection. The trilogy points us to love as the central theme of Christian life, calls us to effective service and revolutionizes our lives so that they are consistent and productive.

*"Immensely readable and full of the practical aspects of spiritual principles."*

Evangelism Today

*"A wealth of good material."*

Martin Goldsmith,
*Church of England Newspaper*

Over 100,000 copies sold.

**George Verwer is the founder and International Director of Operation Mobilisation. He has an international preaching ministry based in Britain.**

OM
publishing

# Serving as Senders

## Neal Pirolo

*ISBN 1-85078-199-0*

"This key book makes the point that mobilizers – the senders – are as crucial to the cause of missions as frontline missionaries. It is a book just crammed with solid, exciting insights on the most hurting link in today's mission movement."

Ralph Winter
*U.S. Centre for World Mission*

"Unless the Church and God's people respond to this book's message, the work of reaching the unreached is going to be greatly hindered. Every committed sender needs to get involved in distributing this book."

George Verwer
*Operation Mobilisation*

**Neal Pirolo is the founding Director of Emmaus Road International, San Diego, California, mobilizing churches, training cross-cultural teams, and networking fellowships with national ministries around the world.**

**OM
publishing**

# Future Leader

## Viv Thomas

*ISBN 0-85364-949-9*

Leadership is a key to success in any organisation.

All the more reason to get it right, says Viv Thomas in a book that sets out to discern the kind of leadership that is needed as we enter a new millennium.

Drawing on biblical models and organisational management research, along with personal experience of some of the evangelical world's most influential leaders, the author provides a model of leadership that is:

- Driven by compassion, not obsession.
- Rooted in relationships, not systems.
- Promotes life, not self-image.

If we fail in these areas, he argues, most of what we do in terms of goals, strategies, skills, mission and communication will eventually be blown away.

This stimulating and inspiring book will test all that might aspire to lead.

**Viv Thomas is the International Co-ordinator of Leadership Development with Operation Mobilisation. He has a world-wide preaching and teaching ministry, with an emphasis on developing leaders. He is also a visiting lecturer at All Nations Christian College in Hertfordshire.**

paternoster
press